MIDDLE CHILD

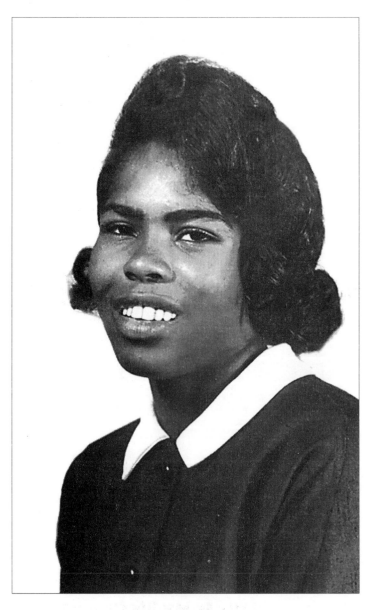

Barbara, age 16

MIDDLE CHILD

This Is My Story

Barbara Booker Wood

✳✳✳✳✳

This book is dedicated to the loving memory of my late parents, Roger Lee and Beulah Hayes Booker, in appreciation of the many sacrifices they made to provide a Christian home filled with love for our family and many other people. Also, this book is dedicated to several people I love who touched my life in a very special way: Aunt Ellen York, mother's only surviving sister; cousin, Edna Giles Smith of Baltimore, Maryland; neighbor, Mother Pearl Robinson; and to the memory of an endearing cousin, Mary Elizabeth Smith of Fort Washington, Maryland, who always provided me with words of wisdom.

✳✳✳✳✳

Foreword

"Middle Child," by Barbara Booker Wood, is a delightful read, one that embraces homespun warmth, the essence of unfettered love, nostalgia, and intrigue.

A first-time author, Mrs. Wood shows incredible talent for remembering incidents that influenced her life as the third of five children (two older, two younger) born to Roger Lee and Beulah Hayes Booker in the unpretentious town of Midlothian, Virginia, a hamlet located approximately 15 miles west of Richmond.

The story she weaves tells of her close family ties, of a way of life barely known about by youngsters of today: ice boxes with drip-pans underneath in the modest home; of school days when teachers were permitted to discipline misbehaving kids without fear of official or parental repercussions.

Then comes the intrigue - a late night elopement to pursue a love bitterly opposed by her parents.

She recalls the ensuing loneliness and economic frustration living in a strange city with no job to contribute to the meagre earnings of a struggling husband.

Eventually, a small job that was nurtured into one of importance and societal acceptance.

Finally, a reconciliation with family and church that subsequently leads to a broader view of her ancestral ties - a pleasant, educational tour of Senegal and The Gambia in West Africa.

Barbara Booker Wood, the "Middle Child," should write more.

Sam Lacy
(Society of Professional Journalists)

CONTENTS

Preface

One may ask two questions: who is Barbara Booker Wood, the middle child, and why should I read her life story? The answer is that she's no special person with no special story to reveal, just an ordinary person whose chosen path in life has been richly blessed by God and she felt it not too personal to share the essence of her life. This book is an affirmation that anyone who desires to preserve and reveal one's life can do so.

From time to time, I'd thought about writing a personal account of my life experiences that would serve as a legacy for my children, grandchildren, other family members and posterity. However, I would abandon the idea almost as quickly as I thought about it. It was not until a few years ago, after retiring from the federal government, that I made the decision to write this story.

My need to write this book was promoted by people, mostly individuals I didn't know, who would ask me what kind of work I did. I would respond by stating, "I'm retired." Immediately, they followed with a second question, asking how I managed to retire early. They would say, "Tell me about your life." I responded that I tried to do what was right by working diligently to accomplish the goals I set for myself. More and more questions would follow and I found myself constantly telling my life story. It was the combination of talking with encouraging people and always wanting to document my life for the generations to follow that made me start writing.

This book is not an expose, nor will it detail every experience in my life. When I examine my birth order, I know that God chose the path for me and He has been with me through it all. God has a purpose and a plan for my life for which I am deeply humbled. I'm glad that I am who I am, born when I was born; not the first, second, fourth or fifth, but the third; the middle child in my family. Growing up in the racially segregated South had a profound effect on my life. It was a period in time when most people looked out for each other, worked hard, and valued family. My prayer is that after you read this book, you, too, will understand your Divine reason for living in your specific time and your birth order, especially, if you are the middle child in your family. You may also be inspired to share your life story with others. May God bless you always.

Acknowledgments

First and foremost, I give honor to my Lord and Savior Jesus Christ for giving me many blessings along my life's journey. Many people helped to bring this book to fruition. Among those, whom I treasure and give credit for their enormous contributions in helping me document my life story, are my closest family members and friends.

So very many people are deserving of thanks for providing love and support to me while working on this project. I'm very appreciative of my siblings: Carol, James, Floyd and Gloria. Thanks to my husband, Claven Sr.; my sons: Claven Jr. and Calvin; my grandchildren: Calvin Jr. and Carmela, and my goddaughter, Tammi. I acknowledge and give praise to a dear family friend, Maretta Hemsley, for the special acts of kindness she contributed to make the book possible. Also, I owe a debt of gratitude to several nieces: Carol (Pinkey), Wanda, and Joy who constantly kept in touch with me to provide words of encouragement. To nephews; Michael (Tony) and Andre, I thank you for your support. To family and friends unmentioned by name, your unconditional love and encouragement helped me to see this project through to the end. God knows your name.

I'm grateful for the prayers and encouragement from my church family, Pastor Jonathan L. Weaver and the members of Greater Mt. Nebo African Methodist Episcopal Church in Upper Marlboro, Maryland. I'm also grateful for the prayers and encouragement of Elder James Quarles, Pastor of Praise Temple Church in Washington, D.C., his wife Gloria, (my younger sister), as well as all of the church members. Lastly, I'm thankful for my final editors and for my publisher.

PART ONE

My Family

My parents, Roger Lee and Beulah Hayes Booker, met, fell in love and married very early in their lives. Both grew up in large families in the same rural area of Virginia, and each had ten siblings. My father, the first of eleven children, was born May 12, 1913, to Willie and Pinkie Booker in a place called Nottoway County, Virginia. I can't recall any memories of my paternal grandparents. My father had seven sisters and three brothers: Sallie, Bertha, Arlene, Malinda, Willie, Frances, Catherine, Leroy, Robert James, and Hallie.

Mother, the youngest of eleven children, was born January 18, 1919, to Richard and Barbery Hayes of Amelia County, Virginia. Her mother died when she was ten years old. Her father, Grandpa Hayes, as we lovingly called him, died during my early years, but I remember him as a kind and gentle man, who was meticulous in his dress. Mother had four sisters and six brothers: Floyd, Joseph, Emma, Annie, Willie, Richard, Mary Alice, Robert, Ellen and Arthur.

When my maternal grandmother, Barbery Hayes, died, my mother was left to be reared by her two older sisters, Emma and Alice. Aunt Emma was already married and had several children of her own, but provided care for my mother in addition to her own children. She lived to be ninety-nine years old. Aunt Alice also helped to care for my mother during her childhood.

1

My father, about twenty years old, left home to take a job in Mansboro (Amelia County), Virginia. Shortly thereafter, he met a young man named Arthur, who introduced him to his youngest sister, Beulah. This is how my father and mother met. While courting my mother, he introduced his younger sister Bertha to Arthur. This introduction also led to romance and marriage—marriages that each lasted over sixty years.

In the mid 1930's, my father did not own a car, so he would walk three or four miles to court my mother. In an interview for this book, I asked my Aunt Bertha, "Who had married first and had the four of you double dated?" I was told my parents were the first to marry on March 6, 1935, when my father was twenty-two and mother only sixteen. Two years later, on February 27, 1937, Uncle Arthur at age nineteen, married Aunt Bertha who was only fifteen. They became my double aunt and uncle, which made their four children, Louise, Arthur Lee, Marvin (deceased) and Robert, my double first cousins. It was customary during the 1930's that most African American people married early, usually in their teens and without a wedding. These days, it's difficult to even think of marrying as young as fifteen. Aunt Bertha and Uncle Arthur never moved away from Amelia County, but my parents moved to Petersburg. The geographical distance between my family and my cousins did not keep us from growing up together. We visited each other often.

After two of years of marriage, my parents had their first child, Carol, born December 9, 1938. Four other children followed, with me as the middle child. I have an older sister and brother, Carol and James, and a younger sister and brother, Margie Gloria and Floyd. By the time I was born in 1942, the family had moved from Petersburg to Midlothian, Virginia. This small community is located approximately fifteen miles west of

Richmond. I was born at home, as were my siblings, and was delivered by a midwife. When I was about six years old, the family moved from Midlothian to Bon Air, where I spent my early years. Bon Air is a small community (just outside of Richmond's city limits) consisting of mostly African American people. By today's standards, our family of seven would have been considered poor; however, we didn't know it, because we always had food, shelter, and clothing.

We lived in a small house on Bon Air Road, which my father built with the help of our neighbors. Our house was made of cinder blocks. It had a small kitchen with a wood/coal burning stove, a cupboard, a small table with a few chairs, a small living room and a couple of bedrooms. Furniture was sparse. There was a time when we had no indoor plumbing, electricity or running water. These things came later. My two sisters and I shared one bedroom and bed, while my two brothers shared another.

My father was an unskilled laborer and mother supplemented his income by working as a domestic: washing, ironing and cleaning white people's houses. She also took care of the white folks children. One family, who employed my mother as a domestic, was the Chamberlains. During this era, most white people weren't known for their generosity toward African Americans, but the Chamberlain family members displayed a sense of warmth toward our family. My mother and my sisters felt affection for Mrs. Chamberlain because of her kindness to our family. I didn't share the feeling, and I don't believe that my father and brothers did, either. While I didn't know the meaning at the time, I viewed the relationship between the two families as unequal, superior and inferior, even though Mrs. Chamberlain sometimes bought us Christmas gifts and school supplies. I never liked going to her house, because we had to enter through the back door. If they came to pick Mother up for work, we had to sit in the back seat of the car. As I think back, I believe we were told to sit in the back seat of the car and enter the house through the back door to make sure we knew we were not equal.

Mother was the kind of person who would do more than what was required, so I believe she was underpaid for her labor. She knew I didn't like going with her to work. She would ask me to help her by doing some of the light work like folding clothes and washing the dishes. My sister, Gloria, six years younger than me, who often went to work with mother, would play with the Chamberlain grandchildren while Mother and I worked. I respected Mother for doing an honest day's work, but I knew I would do something else to earn a living. Mother realized I didn't like doing work at our house and didn't want to work at white people's houses, either. As a child, I was rebellious; and when Mother tried to get me in line, it took a lot. I was quick to complete my assigned chores, and quickness to Mother often meant it was too quick to be done correctly.

Together, my parent's incomes were minimal. Sometimes, my father was between jobs and my mother's income was all the family had to live on. Mother was good at stretching the family's limited income to make ends meet. We were never without food, clothing or other life necessities. On the contrary, we were always feeding and entertaining family and friends. We always helped other people.

Life in our house was pleasant and rather peaceful, even though my father would sometimes drink alcohol. He was also addicted to cigarettes for a number of years. I remember him making many trips to the store to buy his favorite brand, Chesterfield. I cannot remember my father ever drinking alcohol in the presence of his children and he was not

4

a heavy drinker. Mother, a very religious and outspoken woman, would fuss at him when he drank and this led to quarrels between them. I believe if she had said nothing, they would not have argued.

We always had family members visit us, especially on Sundays, to eat, laugh and talk about life. One first cousin, Joyce Booker Worsham (our fathers were brothers) told me that when she visited us as a child, she felt our home was almost like a sacred place. She said she knew there would be no drinking of alcohol, no smoking, no cussing, no playing cards, and my mother would be talking about the Lord. Mother was a missionary, who freely shared God's Word with anyone in her presence. She established rules for our home which, she made sure, were followed by all. Joyce also recalled Mother not allowing anyone to sit on her bed. I don't know why Mother had such strong feelings about this, but everyone knew not to sit on her bed.

To this day, I can't understand how my parents were able to feed and entertain such large numbers of people. Mother sometimes started preparing Sunday's dinner on Saturday evenings and would be cooking late into the night. On Sundays, we ate in shifts and our house could have very easily been called "Booker's All You Can Eat House." Mother was so busy cooking for others that she rarely sat down to eat. We washed a lot of dishes in between servings, because we had no paper or plastic products. Mother was known, in the family and throughout our community, for her delicious homemade rolls, biscuits and scrumptious fried chicken. Everyone claimed her fried chicken was the best they had ever eaten. Some family members even brought their food to our house so Mother could cook it.

Most of our fruit came from our apple and peach trees in our backyard. And, we also had grapevines that produced the sweetest grapes. It was so much fun to pick and eat them. We did not live on a farm, but we did grow a lot of the food we ate. My brothers, as little boys, were made to dig up potatoes and pick corn from the field, which would later be cooked for our meals. My father raised chickens and pigs. In order to kill the chickens for cooking, father would break their necks and then throw them on the ground to die. This was scary and it made me sad to watch the chickens flutter around on the ground taking several minutes to die. After the chickens were dead, we had to scald them with hot water and pick off the feathers. I didn't want to eat them after seeing how they were killed, but it was a part of our meals. We were made to do our share of the work that was necessary for our family's survival. Being the middle child and often overlooked in the family, I wasn't called on to do some of the chores.

As I grew up I noticed my father and mother had each other, my older siblings, Carol and James (Jimmy) bonded together, as did my younger siblings, Gloria and Floyd. I tended to stay close to Mother, because of my siblings' relationships with each other. I felt like the odd one in the family always trying to find a place for myself. Acting a little stubborn and attempting to have the last word were my ways of trying to gain some attention.

Psychologists have characterized the middle child in many different ways. Some say we are sociable and outgoing, yet also quiet and somewhat shy, a rebel and a peacemaker, aggressive, but wanting to avoid conflicts. From time to time all of these characteristics fit my personality. Usually, I tried to make the situation, whatever it was, work for me. I attempted to dominate my parents and my siblings. I was unable to clearly express my desire for more attention from my parents and they seemed unaware of how I felt.

Our family had a pet like most typical families in the neighborhood did. We had a tiny black and white dog named "Snoopy." I loved him. However, Mother would not allow him inside our house. One of her rules was that the dog should be outside in his own house.

Throughout our neighborhood, there were a lot of men who passed by our door during the week. They provided us with services and conveniences. I remember when the breadman and the milkman came by to sell and deliver their products. During my early years, refrigerators were not common in most homes. Most families used iceboxes instead. The iceman would drive around the neighborhood selling ice by the pound from the back of his truck about twice a week. We would use a pick to chop off pieces for our use. Our water supply came from a well in our backyard. Brothers, Floyd and Jimmy, would draw buckets and buckets of water for all of our needs, including our weekly bathing.

Mother taught us some things about cooking, but she preferred to cook the family meals herself. I just could not cook to her satisfaction and I really don't think I tried as hard as I could have. She was a perfectionist; and we girls rarely pleased her. When I was assigned the chore of peeling potatoes, snapping string beans or washing greens, Mother would complain that I wasted the potatoes by peeling them too thick, that I snapped the beans too long or wasted usable greens. Sometimes, my thoughts were, "If you don't like the way I am doing this, why not do it yourself?" Of course, I never spoke those words, because I loved and respected my mother. There were hard times for our family; however, we managed the best we could with what we had.

As for clothing, I wore my sister's hand-me-downs. I had no choice in the matter whatsoever. I remember complaining to my mother how unfair it was, when my older sister, Carol, got new clothes, that I was expected to wear her old ones while my younger sister, Gloria, also got new clothes. One reason Gloria got new clothes was because Carol and I had worn out the old ones before they could be passed down to her. Mother purchased the dresses at a cost of $10 (for two or three) from Sears or Rayless Department Store on Broad Street in Richmond.

My memories of a typical Sunday at our house meant all seven of our family members would gather at the breakfast table to enjoy a meal of fish and fried potatoes along with homemade biscuits. Mother would read passages from the Bible and we would have family prayer. After breakfast, we would get dressed and attend Sunday school and church service at Mt. Nebo. Sunday service could be heard for some distance with preaching and singing that blended together into a spiritual high. After church, the children would go outside and play until the family dinner was ready.

My mother and father were devout Baptists and during my early years, made churchgoing mandatory in our house. I'm grateful because it helped to shape who I am today. The little country church (Mt. Nebo) located alongside Bon Air Road was directly across from our house. My father served as a custodian for the church.

On New Year's Eve, we usually attended what we called Watch Night Service. My family, along with some of the other families in our community, had the old-fashioned belief (suspicion) that a male should be the first person to enter the house on New Year's Day to bring good luck for the rest of the year. Because of this belief, one of the deacons or another man from the church would come to our house directly after the service to be our first visitor of the year.

During my teen years, my parents shifted religious allegiance from the Baptist to the Pentecostal church. Led by Mother, the family started attending church in Richmond, at Refuge Church, under the Organization of the Church of Our Lord Jesus Christ. Bishop John W. Pernell became their pastor. However, I remember we still attended services at Mt. Nebo also. Mother had a lovely voice and enjoyed singing songs of praise to God. Often, she would sing and read the Bible late at night. I believe she sang to make herself happy.

One of Mother's favorite songs was written by Bishop Pernell and is titled "Let Me Live by Thy Word Every Day." She had no professional training as a singer, but she could match any professional when she lifted her voice during this song. She became very popular, and numerous requests were made for her to sing this song in many different churches. Her spirit of joy, enthusiasm and love for God gave my life impetus. I had one of the greatest mothers God ever gave anyone. She was a woman of strong faith and an optimist, who believed and trusted God for everything. She wouldn't hesitate to tell anyone if she felt that they were involved in what she thought was ungodly behavior. I believe it was partly because of her daily sermons that, after many years, my father gave up his habits of smoking and occasional drinking to become a dedicated doorkeeper and a deacon in his church. Both of my parents extended kindness and generosity to the people they met.

Throughout their lives, my parents served the Lord. And, their last years were spent working diligently within the Church of Our Lord Jesus Christ of the Apostolic Faith, Inc., under the leadership of Bishop William L. Bonner. In November 1978, God blessed my parents with a trip to the Holy Land. They traveled with the Bishop and others. This

9

experience was a highlight of their lives. Until his death, my father would say to people, "I've walked in Jerusalem just like John." He talked of how he stepped in the Jordan River and about the prayers that he said at the Wailing Wall.

My father died in April 1990, and my mother died in January 1996. They were married for over sixty years. While there were challenges in their marriage, I know they loved each other. My father would sometimes speak of how pretty he thought Mother was, especially as a young girl, and he often talked about her lovely figure.

A long-time family friend, Virginia Brown, shared with me that she enjoyed the hospitality my parents provided her, especially when she visited their home on Sundays after the church service. She said, "I sensed that they respected and cared for each other." My youngest brother, Floyd, aware of the closeness between our parents, insisted at their deaths that their remains be placed at the same site. Floyd said, "They stayed together in life, let's not separate them in death." As a result, my parents are buried together at Jerusalem Baptist Church in Nottoway County, Virginia, the boyhood church of my father and his family. My mother's childhood church is Manassa Hill Baptist in Amelia County, Virginia, just a short distance away.

Early Childhood Years

Growing up as the middle child in a large family, in the rural community of Bon Air, Virginia, was an experience for which I am thankful. Most of my childhood was spent right in my neighborhood, except for occasional trips to the beach on the Eastern Shore of Virginia, a few church-sponsored trips to other parts of the county and weekend visits to Amelia County to visit relatives. My life was centered on the church, the place where I received instructions for life and the social place for gatherings in the community.

I remember the summer days of outdoor play and the cool nights of running barefoot in our yard or the neighbor's, catching lightning bugs with no fear of harm. We usually played outside until it was dark. All of the children who lived on Bon Air Road and Robious Road played together and attended the same school. As I recall, only a few households had a telephone or a television set, but almost every house had a radio.

The two radio stations that my family listened to were WANT and WRVA. WANT was the number one station for gospel music and church broadcasts on Sundays, while WRVA gave us the news. My older sister, Carol, worked as the secretary at WANT while she was a student at Virginia Union University. Since most of us did not have a television to keep us inside and away from each other, we usually played outside under the watchful view of an adult.

Our neighborhood was made up of a mix of people from various walks of life, professional and non-professional. We had the usual problems and concerns, the same as in other communities. I recall a man named Mr. Steele, who from time to time would get inebriated, stand by his mailbox on the side of the road and talk to it for hours. He didn't bother anyone; we children would look at him and laugh. We thought his behavior was strange. I realize now that there were many benefits of growing up in a small community of all African American people, who cared for one another and shared time together. The memories of one elementary school teacher, Miss Winston, and our principal, Mrs. Scott, who lived just a few houses from us, are very vivid. Both believed and enforced strict discipline with students. In Bon Air, there was truly a sense of community among the people. Another neighbor, Mrs. Charlotte Day, was the community's beautician for many years. Everyone knew everyone and what they were doing. Actually, the neighborhood was like one large family living in separate houses. We didn't have to be concerned about keeping a key to our house, because most of the time we didn't lock our doors, except at night. Mt. Nebo Baptist Church was the sustaining force in our community that held families together sharing and caring for each other and enjoying life together.

For me, as well as most of the other children in the community, there was no question about attending church on Sunday. Not only was attendance a must, but the proper attire was also required, especially for the girls. Mother would press and tightly curl our hair or she would send us to Mrs. Day for the same so we would be ready for Sunday. The ladies of the church led by example, wearing hats and gloves. Most of us wore white gloves and the same hat almost every Sunday, because we had so few. The dresses we wore were always starched and ironed. Today, women's attire for Sunday service is vastly different from when I grew up. Seldom do I see women wearing long white gloves or women and children regularly wearing hats. In my youth, I looked forward to Christmas and other special occasions, because the children got a chance to actively take part in church programs. We participated in drama presentations, where we had to know our parts to perfection. It was the church, not Toastmasters, (that came later in my federal government career), where I first received public speaking lessons. I recall Mt. Nebo's annual Spring revivals, which gathered people together, children and adults, to hear fiery sermons and to help others make the decision to confess their faith in God. During this period, revivals were the only times I remember people being offered the opportunity to confess their faith. Today most, if not all churches regardless of the denomination, usually provide the opportunity at any service and even during funerals. During the revivals at Mt. Nebo, a special area, usually the front row of the church was reserved and referred to as the mourner's bench. If it was your year, as determined by your parents or a surrogate, you had to sit on the mourner's bench throughout the revival, until you made your public confession. While on the mourner's bench, the preacher and deacons would pray over you. Once you made your confession and acknowledged your belief, the prayer of salvation would be offered with you.

At age twelve, I went to the mourner's bench, acknowledged my belief and confessed my faith. Reverend Peter Ross was the Pastor of Mt. Nebo at the time of my religious experience. The next step was the baptismal service, held annually on the third Sunday in June. Dressed in white from head to toe, I was immersed in water in the outdoor pool of

13

the church. I don't recall how many other people, having confessed their belief, were baptized with me, but I remember there were several neighborhood children and an adult or two. I no longer see or hear people talking about the mourner's bench and it is my belief that this tradition has been replaced in most churches with an altar call or what we now refer to as "opening the doors of the church." One thing that hasn't changed is the prayer of salvation, which is still offered with new converts. My parents were happy when I went to the mourner's bench. In spite of my confession, I was still the little girl who loved to laugh and talked more than some adults felt that I should.

The security I felt in my home was also felt throughout our neighborhood, because the older people took special interest in the children and protected us. They expected certain behavior from us and it was understood that they had permission to reprimand and chastise us for any inappropriate behavior they observed.

Some studies report that the middle child frequently struggles for attention and a place in the family. Early in my life, I tended to stick close to my mother in search of my place in the family, but she was too busy looking out for the good of the entire family to provide the special attention I sought. She would often give me a brief moment of attention and then she was off to do what she felt was necessary for the whole family. It has been further stated that the middle child would feel unloved in the home. I didn't feel unloved. I saw that my parents had their own way of showing all of us their love and I felt loved by many other family members and friends. I can't recall my father ever verbalizing his love, but he expressed it in different ways. When the adults from Mt. Nebo Church: Sunday School teachers, deacons, and other people, praised us and informed our father of how well-behaved and attentive we were at church and on church sponsored trips, I could see the pride in his eyes. Both parents showed their love and pride in us when we shared our accomplishments in school with them. As I interviewed my siblings for this book, they didn't agree with my perception of often being left out by them during play. Nevertheless, I know what I experienced as a result of my birth order.

As a little girl, my small rubber doll was my constant companion. Unlike the children today, who get many toys during the period of one year, Christmas was the only time that most of us got a toy. We appreciated the one toy that we received because it had to last until the next Christmas.

I remember how my parents, teachers and others in our community stressed that education was essential. They often spoke of a brighter future and the value of an education. Our teachers taught us in such a special way that we could sense their desire for us to achieve. My parents, as did most parents, supported the teachers in the punishments we received at school and further discipline would follow at home as reinforcement. As I recall, it was mostly the boys that got punished; the girls were usually spared — at least, I was.

My formal education began at Midlothian Elementary School in the town of Midlothian, the place of my birth. This meant that we had to be bused to school. My older siblings attended a little wooden school named Mt. Nebo, which was within walking distance of our house. The year I reached age six and was ready for school, Mt. Nebo merged with several other African American schools, and all students were sent to Midlothian Elementary School. The other schools that were part of the merger were Spring Creek and Robious. Research revealed that the original Midlothian School was a log building built in 1877 on land belonging to the Midlothian African Church on Westfield Drive. In 1948, Midlothian had approximately 200 students ranging in grades one through seven. We did not have Middle or Junior High School during this period. Instead, when we completed elementary, we went directly to high school. I was excited about going to school, but I recall being somewhat apprehensive about how things would be. I enjoyed school, because I loved reading and writing. I loved to recite in class and enjoyed our spelling lessons. I was a good student in elementary school and I am certain that my birth order had an impact on my performance as it reflected my personality.

The only behavior problem reported to my parents from teachers was for talking more than I should. Mother would instruct me to stop talking so much in school, but I would convince her that the reports did not reflect my performance or my behavior. My parents never questioned the teachers, but my middle child personality allowed me to get out of most sticky situations. I tried to dominate the teachers, but was unsuccessful. I was made to walk the line the same as the other students, especially with Miss Winston. She seemed always to be watching me and would say, "Girl, you will not get away with this...." She was so tough on me. It wasn't long before I realized that I had no choice but to follow her rules. Miss Winston was the person who first labeled me the "middle child". She would tell my parents that they should pay more attention to their middle child. I sensed she was concerned I might get into trouble, because of the lack of attention from them.

During my elementary school days, only three girls were in my first grade class: Ruby Brown, Lucille Turner, and me. Ruby and I knew each other from the neighborhood. Mr. Walter and Mrs. Dorothy, her parents, were friends with my parents. We met Lucille at school and the three of us became close friends. People met one another during these days and there was instantaneous friendship. Lucille's mother, also called Mrs. Dorothy, by us children, didn't live in the Bon Air community, but she soon joined the family friendship. While I loved reading and writing, arithmetic was not one of my favorite subjects. It didn't matter, because Ruby was there to provide whatever help I needed. Today, I think of my friend, Ruby Brown Wallace, with many happy memories of our childhood days - playing in our neighborhood, attending Sunday school and church at Mt. Nebo, entering Midlothian Elementary and Carver High School together. I am saddened that I'm unable to communicate with her, because a severe disability has caused her to be unable to talk or to walk. Her mother told me that Ruby's major accomplishment was to earn a Master's Degree from William and Mary College, Williamsburg, Virginia, during a period in her life when a disability made it difficult for her to walk and impossible to write. All of her classroom lectures were taped, and all of her tests were oral. In spite of Ruby's health challenge, her high academic achievements were remarkable. God blessed her with fortitude to continue her education and graduate with honors. She has been confined to her bed for almost thirty years now. However, her family - mother, sister and husband are lovingly caring for her. I can't think of my childhood days in Bon Air without thinking of Ruby and our close friendship.

Arriving home after school meant we had to complete some chores around the house. My brothers did the outdoor chores, like taking care of the animals and working in the garden, while my sisters and I did the indoor chores of cleaning and ironing. Only after our tasks were completed were we permitted to go outside to play. We entertained ourselves by playing hopscotch, dodge ball, jump rope, marbles, jack-rocks and hide-

and-seek, among other games. We organized our games and got along pretty well. We learned about leadership, sharing and cooperation by playing these games. Any differences that came up were settled amongst ourselves. I can't recall getting into a real fight (maybe a fuss or two) with some of the neighborhood children. When our parents gave us money, we would walk to Ruby's uncle's (Mr. Tom Brown) store to buy candy. He was a respected deacon in our church and was very kind to the children. He would give us candies sometimes when we didn't have any money to pay. Our family shopping was done at Siegel's Supermarket in South Richmond.

We children were all members of a national religious organization called the Good Samaritan State Grand Lodge, which was headquartered in Richmond, Virginia, with chapters throughout Chesterfield County, the state of Virginia and beyond. Our chapter was referred to as Mt. Nebo's Juvenile Chapter. The Good Samaritan Lodge operated along the lines of the biblical teachings of helping those in need. As members, we were required to pay dues, which was about five cents per meeting. These get-togethers were held in a little wooden building within walking distance of our house, called the Lodge. I enjoyed my participation in this organization and can remember people, like Messrs. Earl Johnson, Emmett Gregory and his wife Alberta. They were the leaders who directed our programs and activities. The men were deacons in our church, and all of the adults at the Lodge were members of Mt. Nebo. Mr. Emmett was, during my youth and is still today, a pillar of the church and the Bon Air community. When I reflect upon my youthful days, I think of two special adults from the community who provided love, encouragement and support to me: Mr. Emmett and Alberta. While they never had any children of their own, they served as surrogate parents to many children in the community. My love for them along with their love for me, and my family, remains in tact today.

Looking back over the years, I realize my upbringing, especially my parent's guidance, the strong spiritual influence of Mt. Nebo Baptist Church and the love, support and encouragement from teachers and others were the driving forces in my life. I unconsciously made the decision never to let these people down. Consequently, I never took to smoking or drinking alcohol nor engaged in other destructive behaviors. I've always wanted to live up to my parents' teachings of being honest and upright. What I learned growing up in Bon Air, Virginia, is more valuable than any amount of money I could ever have. I grew up at a time when it was honorable to try to live life by the Golden Rule. I close this chapter on my early years, which forever shaped my character, stating that I am indebted to my parents for their living example and my extended family — the village people of Bon Air—who in many, many ways nurtured me.

Teen Years through High School

My eighth grade classmates from Midlothian Elementary and I were excited the day we arrived at Carver High School. This racially segregated high school was named in honor of the well-known scientist, George Washington Carver. The school was a little two-story brick building that included thirteen classrooms built for a capacity of 350 students. However, when my class arrived in September 1955, the total student population was 562. Carver was located in Chester, approximately thirty miles from my home in Bon Air.

Carver High opened its doors in 1948, only seven years prior to my enrollment, with 347 students. It began as a result of the consolidation of Hickory Hill High, located in the northern section of Chesterfield County, and D. Webster Davis High School, which was on the campus of Virginia State College. It included grades eight through twelve. Students were bused from all areas of Chesterfield County to Carver, the only high school in the county for African American students. Our school operated with insufficient funding and second-hand books. Nevertheless, Carver's faculty was made up of dedicated teachers who taught us we that could achieve and be first-class citizens.

Upon arriving at Carver High on a yellow school bus driven by Mr. Levi Johnson of Midlothian, I met many teenagers from various schools throughout Chesterfield County. My class was made up of 130 students.

Wilma Hubbard was one of the first students I met at Carver and she became my life long friend. I later made friends with Phoebe, Shirley, Ruth Ella, Hazel, Nina, Mary, Lillie, Doris, Edna, Forrest Mae and many other classmates.

Prior to my high school days I used my middle name, Evelyn. When I arrived at Carver, the teachers started referring to me by my first name, Barbara. My friend and classmate, Lucille, found herself in the same situation. The teachers began referring to her, using her first name, Eleanor. Her family, and those who knew her prior to high school, continued to call her Lucille. Neither of us wanted to tell our teachers not to use our first name, so we answered by both. Even to this day we answer by both. When she hears Lucille and I hear Evelyn, we know it's family or someone who knew us before our days at Carver.

My oldest sister, Carol, four years ahead of me in school, graduated in Carver's Class of 1956. We shared one year of high school together. My brother James was two years ahead of me; however, I caught up with him and we were both in the ninth grade at the same time. School was fun and I greatly enjoyed my teen years and high school days. I know that I could have applied myself better in school, but I was interested in other things, which I sometimes put ahead of my studies. God blessed me and I did not have to repeat any year.

I especially enjoyed English and Literature, because I enjoyed reading and writing. I would read whatever books or papers I could find. At home, there were only a few books and magazines. Of course, we had the Bible, our Sunday school book, a dictionary and a book or two about Booker T. Washington, Frederick Douglass and George Washington Carver. We also often had two newspapers at home: the Richmond Afro

American and the Richmond News Leader. I also had my school textbooks from which to read. When Mother would give us spending money, I would buy magazines such as, True Story, True Confessions and Modern Romance.

Some of the teachers at Carver took a special interest in me as a student and provided encouragement and support. They were Messrs. Williams, Suggs and Cook. Also, Mrs. Barnes and Mrs. Eskridge gave me special attention. Each year my class lost some of its students either because families moved away or students dropped out of school. By the time we became juniors, our numbers had dropped from 130 to 87. By then, Mrs. Eskridge was known for her special way of calling some of us girls "little frisky pieces." I think she referred to us using this term because we were, or seemed to be, more interested in music, clothes, make-up and talking with the boys than in the Social Studies lesson she taught.

The school gave demerits for misconduct. I don't recall ever receiving any demerits for inappropriate behavior because, most of the time, I tried to stay out of trouble and did what was required.

Our school had numerous extra-curricular activities for its students. Carver's philosophy was to develop the students academically, physically, culturally and socially, as well as morally. I especially enjoyed my participation in these organizations: the Future/New Homemakers of America, the Library Club, the Future Business Leaders of America and the Choir. I also enjoyed being a Cheerleader.

In addition to my school and church activities, like most teenagers, I had a few teenage idols. Some of them were The Flamingos, whose very popular song was "I Only Have Eyes For You;" Sam Cooke, known for "You Send Me;" Jackie Wilson (Mr. Entertainment) most popular song

"Lonely Teardrops;" Gene Chandler; known for, "The Duke of Earl" and Jerry (The Ice Man) Butler popular song "For Your Precious Love." I enjoyed listening and dancing to the music of my teen years.

While the average student population of Carver was approximately 500, there existed groupology among the students, faculty and administrators. Groupology is my word to describe groups within groups. For the most part, students who had the same interests grouped themselves together. On a small scale, the light and dark skin issue existed in our school environment, starting in the principal's office. Mr. Brown, our principal, and some faculty members provided certain favors to those students who could pass the "lighter than brown paper bag test." Mr. Brown's own skin color could not pass the test, but it appeared that he favored those persons whose skin color was unlike his and could pass the test. I was not disturbed by the skin color issue, which existed at Carver because my middle child personality allowed me to make the best from any situation. My personality in my family culture carried over into the school climate to do what I had to, regardless of the issue. I expressed myself without disrespect for our principal, teachers or students, and, even in my youth, I insisted upon respect in return.

One situation I vividly recall from my high school days centered around an opportunity some of us had to appear on television. To discuss this particular situation, I'll refer to Carver students as Group A and Group B. With the approval of our principal and accompanied by school faculty, Group A students made an appearance on television, representing our school. Sometime later, Group B students, myself included, also had an opportunity to be on television. Our appearance was to take place on a local television dance program, which spun off from the national dance show called "American Bandstand," hosted by Dick Clark. The Richmond area local dance show was called "Teen Age Party," hosted by Jesse Duboy and aired weekly on WRVA Channel 12. We were so excited about this opportunity, even more excited than many of us had ever been in our lives. Mr. Brown decided that Group B students could not go on television. When he informed us of his decision, we refused to accept it and were determined to go anyway. While our principal gave us no reason for his decision, I had my own idea about why he took the position that he did. As I reflect back on the matter, we had a lot of guts to go against our principal. However, even as a teenager, I knew that he was wrong to attempt to prevent us from making a television appearance, when he had earlier permitted the other group to go. At the same time that we were working to make sure that our principal did not stop our appearance, I was faced with the challenge to convince my parents to allow me to go. Mother didn't see dancing as Godly behavior. However, I knew if I could get my father to approve then she would agree.

Phoebe, the planner and organizer of the event, was determined that we would appear on the show, because she wanted to sing. Phoebe lived with her uncle, Rev. Truehart (a Baptist preacher), because her parents were deceased. I don't think her uncle believed much in this kind of hoopla, but he granted her permission anyway. Gloria and Lewis, Phoebe's sister and brother also received permission to appear on the show. I told my parents the show was a school sponsored event and a part of our assignment, so they granted me the permission I needed. This was the biggest lie I ever told my parents and I felt guilty about it. After much convincing, the school did provide us with transportation. We danced to Chubby Checker's song, the "Twist," did the "Loco Motion" and the

"Stroll," just as the young people did on "American Bandstand." Phoebe had her opportunity to sing on television. Our television appearance both added to our popularity and created jealousy among our peers.

My family, neighbors from Bon Air, and classmates still talk about the television appearance to this day, some forty years later. We were glad we didn't get into trouble for disobeying our principal and we were also proud we didn't let him take the opportunity from us.

Not only was our school segregated, so were all public facilities and public transportation. We had to sit in the back of the bus and could only use the colored side of the Greyhound bus station when my family made its Saturday trips to downtown Richmond. These were fun trips and I was always excited about going into the city to shop. Mother, my sisters and I would make our weekly trips via the Greyhound bus to downtown Richmond. The station, located on Broad Street, had separate seating areas, bathrooms and water fountains. We had to use the ones labeled "Colored Only." While buying our tickets to ride the bus, I remember the ticket sellers, all white people, being rude and discourteous, making it clear that they did not want to provide service to us because of the color of our skin.

In downtown Richmond, we would shop on Broad Street at Rayless, Woolworth and G.C. Murphy. The two major and expensive stores in the center of the city were Thalhimers and Miller & Rhodes. We could not afford to do much shopping at these stores because the prices were beyond our means, but I remember Thalhimers had a basement that sold cheaper items and when we could, we'd shop there. When mother had extra money, she would buy us hot dogs and sodas at the Murphy or Woolworth counter. The facilities in these stores were also segregated, so we had to stand at the end of the counter to eat our food, even when seats were available. They were reserved for the white people. As a teenager, I knew that this made no sense, because I didn't feel inferior to anyone and I told my mother so. I suppose it was the rebel part of my middle child personality that surfaced on the day that I informed Mother I wanted to occupy one of the empty seats in Woolworth. She quickly admonished me saying, "Stay in your place." It was clear to me that Mother wanted to protect me from what could have happened if I had disobeyed the law. I believe that Mother trusted God to right all wrongs, including racial bigotry. She taught us to respect the law and to respect all people, regardless of their race. Her teaching did not stop me from wanting to challenge the system of racism. I hoped that someday I would be able to do something about the situation. At that time I didn't know that God would later allow me to march in the protest of inequality and injustice with Dr. Martin Luther King, Jr.

Mother provided as best she could for her five children on the family's low income. She was a stickler for our being clean and neatly dressed whenever we went out. When she didn't take my sisters and I to Mrs. Day for our hair care Mother would take us to Arnello's Beauty Shop in downtown Richmond, at Third and Clay Streets. Wherever we went our thick, coarse and long hair was pressed hard and curled tight. I recall the burns I received from the metal straightening comb used on my hair.

Age sixteen was an exciting period in my life. I was permitted far more freedom than my older sister and brother. My dating was vastly different from my older sister's. When Carol was dating, my father insisted that I accompany her on her dates, even though, for the most part, she was only permitted to go to church services or church related programs. We could stop on the way home to get something to eat at fast food places, but we had a curfew time. Carol was the oldest in the family and first to begin dating. My father kept a sharp eye on her.

It was at a church service that Carol met her first boyfriend. He was a handsome man from the Northside section of Richmond named Wilburt Carter. He was friendly, churchgoing and from a prominent Richmond family. There was an instant friendship between his family and ours. Mother took to liking him immediately, because he was connected to church, a gentleman, and he gave us no reason to dislike him. Wilburt was a member of one of Richmond's popular gospel groups called the Celestial Chorus of Shiloh Baptist Church in the Churchill section of the city.

During the beginning of the relationship, my father had serious concerns with Carol's dating because he was so overprotective of her. I didn't want to accompany her on dates and would rather have stayed home to read my books or do what interested me. I had to obey my father though, and I wanted my sister to be happy, so I went with her. Wilburt knew that if I didn't go with them, Carol most likely would not be allowed to go out. So, in order to make me happy, he tried matchmaking. I felt he acted as if he had a special calling to find a boyfriend for me. He came from a large family and had many brothers, so he tried to match me up with his younger brother, Leon. Neither of us was interested in a courting relationship. However, we became friends.

Another of Wilburt's matchmaking attempts was with David Reynolds. Wilburt and David were friends and members the Celestial Chorus. Tall, dark and handsome, David became my friend. The four of us spent time talking at the concerts and eating out at fast food places. On occasions, David would come to my home with Wilburt to visit me. While a real dating relationship never developed between David and I, we were sociable. His parents, Mr. & Mrs. Reynolds, and my parents became friends because of their Christian lifestyle.

During interviews for this book, Wilburt recalled an incident when my father, being so angry to hear that Carol was pregnant, got his shotgun out after him. He said that he and his friend, Herman Lee, also a member of the Celestial Chorus, fled our house on foot leaving the car in our yard. Wilburt said that he loved Carol and would have married her without my father's drastic action.

After things settled down a bit, my family planned a lovely wedding for them. I believe I was just as excited about the wedding as they were. In spite of our limited funds, my parents spent quite a bit of money on the wedding. I was happy to get my gown from Thalhimers, Richmond's exclusive store. This was my first gown. It was a floor-length taffeta one with fishnet overlay. Not only did I get a new gown and serve as Carol's bridesmaid, I also convinced her to let two of my classmates be bridesmaids. So Phoebe and Shirley went to Thalhimers to purchase identical gowns. David's sister, Eula and her husband, Clyde (also members of the Celestial Chorus) attended the wedding.

Wilburt and Carol were married in November of 1958. He continued his singing with Carol by his side. He later joined another one of Richmond's popular gospel groups, the Virginia Chorale Ensemble, and continued spreading the gospel through songs for about eight years. The members of the Virginia Chorale Ensemble were from Cedar Street Baptist Church where Rev. Benjamin W. Robinson, Jr. was, and still is, the Pastor. All of the really good gospel singing in Richmond came from these two groups. The mighty Virginia Chorale Ensemble continues to sing today and is Richmond's leading gospel group.

While Wilburt was singing with the Virginia Chorale Ensemble, he continued his efforts to find a mate for me. At the end of one of the concerts, Wilburt said to me, "I've got someone who is just right for you...I know you'll like him and he'll like you." He introduced me to Arthur (Pap) Braxton, a member of this group, telling each of us how great the other was. It didn't work. Again, his efforts failed to match us as boyfriend and girlfriend, but the two of us spent time together as casual friends attending the group's concerts throughout the Richmond area. Shortly after the marriage, my niece Carol was born and she brought excitement and joy to our entire family.

My first real dating relationship started when I was sixteen. This relationship enriched my life so much that it truly helped to shape who I am today. The relationship grew out of a pen pal friendship. One day as I was reading the Richmond Afro American newspaper, I noticed a section referred to as "Pen Pals." Wanting to expand my world beyond Bon Air, I submitted my name and address as an individual seeking to correspond with other people as pen pals. I became a pen pal with three persons. Two were females, one from Baltimore, Maryland, and the other from Richmond, Virginia. The third person was a male who was residing in Washington, D.C. He was originally from Petersburg, Virginia. The two women did not correspond with me for any length of time, but the third pen pal became my first special friend. His name was John Hardy, Jr. He was a sergeant in the United States Marine Corps and stationed in Washington, D.C.

We communicated with each other through letters, postcards and pictures. After months of sharing so much in our letters, we decided we wanted to meet in person. John's letters were so descriptive of his life and he found my letters interesting enough to continue writing as pen pals. Through his letters, I learned about new places and new experiences. This was a very exciting period in my life. In 1958, when a letter could be mailed with a three-cent stamp, Mother provided me with many stamps to mail my letters to John. Sometime later, the postage increased to five cents. Mother questioned my writing so many letters, but always gave me the stamps. I was not interested in any of the boys at Carver because of my friendship with John. I was infatuated with him and inspired by his writings. I know that my close friends at school heard more about him than they wanted to hear, because he was my main topic of conversation. I was excited about sharing my experiences with my friends. Everything was going great in my life and I was as happy as any teenager could possibly be.

John and I wrote to each other frequently. We shared family stories, our interests and hobbies. He shared stories about his life as a Marine. I shared the experiences of my high school days and life in Bon Air. He was quite a few years my senior and very mature. He shared with me the pain of his divorce and the joys of his two children. He would travel from Washington, D.C. to Petersburg, Virginia to visit his mother and his children.

When he asked if he could come to visit me, I didn't even ask my parents. My letter of response said "Yes!" I had watched my father be extremely hard on my older sister when she started to date and I wondered how my father would handle my dating. He had insisted that I accompany

Carol on her dates, but did not require my younger sister, Gloria, to accompany me. My parents, as well as my siblings, knew about my pen pal relationship with John. I didn't know how to tell them I had invited him to visit me. I wanted to ask for their permission before the day he was supposed to come, but somehow I never did. I did not want to hear "No" as their answer.

The day of his first visit finally arrived and it was a lovely Sunday afternoon during the summer. With all of the people who came through our house, family members by the carloads and other people from the church, I thought he would fit right in with our usual Sunday visitors. I told my younger brother and sister, Floyd and Gloria, that John was coming to visit, but they were ages ten and twelve and weren't interested in what I was planning. On that day, I had attended church, came home and anxiously awaited his arrival. Dressed in my church clothes and very nervous, I watched John drive up to our house in a beautiful 1957 yellow Ford Fairlane 500 with a white convertible top. The car was the prettiest I'd ever seen. There I was inside the house looking out the window, too nervous to even come out to meet him. My father met him in the yard and talked with him first. The usual Sunday visitors were at our house. I felt like I was stuck on the hot seat, but could not move. I wasn't sure he would like me after a meeting me in person. I was afraid I would not meet his expectations.

It seemed like ages passed while I stood in the house and he stood in the yard talking with my father. My father finally came in the house and jokingly said, "Your newspaper boyfriend is here to see you." It was at that point that I had the first face-to-face meeting with John. As I looked into his hazel eyes, I was stunned to see that John looked even

32

more handsome in person than in his picture. John was very comfortable with my family and me. He was extremely friendly and one of the kindest persons I have ever met. I can't remember how long his first visit was, but he never came into the house that day. I entertained him sitting under a tree in our front yard. This was the beginning of a very significant part of my life.

John was about twenty-three years old and had experienced a great deal in life while I was only sixteen with very little experience. My entire family, especially my older sister, Carol, took to John's kind demeanor. He was very reserved and a gentleman to the utmost, which my family recognized right away. He was a non-smoker and a non-drinker. Mother was happy about this. After his first visit, he came almost every other weekend. My parents were very comfortable with our friendship. Because they were at ease with us and busy with the cares of their own lives, they did not pay a lot of attention to our comings and goings.

The neighbors knew all about my relationship with John. I remember Miss Winston, who seemed to keep a close eye on me, telling my mother that she needed to pay more attention to my going out with a strange boy, because he was not from our neighborhood. She'd already labeled me the middle child, who needed to be watched more. I knew she was concerned about me, but I didn't like her close watch on what I was doing. Soon, it became a joke in the family and with some of the neighbors that I ordered my boyfriend from the newspaper. While no one knew John, until he came to see me, everyone who met him quickly became aware of his kind and gentle spirit. John knew that my family greatly admired him and he enjoyed spending time with us. My parents saw that we respected the rules of our home and we never stayed out late. We spent a lot of time together enjoying each other's company.

When I arrived home from school, I would go directly to our mailbox by the side of the road to see if he had written me a letter. At least once or twice a week, there would be mail from him and I was happy. Our first date was to the Bellwood Drive-In Movie Theater on Petersburg Pike. During this era, going to a drive-in movie was customary for young people. We would roll down the window to place a box thereon to hear, while we watched black and white movies on the big screen. We immensely enjoyed each other's company. Romance for us did not go beyond hugs, holding hands and light kissing. John always displayed the greatest respect for me and for our age difference. He said he never wanted to do anything that would prevent me from graduating from high school, because he valued education. I was very naive and probably would have done anything he asked. I can't recall ever a time I was not allowed to go on a date with John. I simply told my parents where we planned to go and permission was granted. By now, Wilburt, had given up on finding someone for me, he accepted and befriended John. Carol and John often wrote letters to one another.

On several of our dates John and I went to Buckroe Beach in the Virginia Tidewater area for the entire afternoon. Buckroe, a totally segregated beach, was the closest one to us. The other beach in the area, Bayshore, was for whites only. I am certain that Buckroe Beach did not have the amenities of Bayshore, but we enjoyed ourselves all the same. John and I would sit on the beach talking, laughing and eating for hours.

On occasion, during my senior year in high school, John would drive twenty miles from his mother's house in Petersburg to Bon Air to take me to school. Some Fridays, he would travel from Washington, D.C. so that he could be at Carver by the end of the school day to take me home. I was truly a happy teenager dating John, and riding around in his beautiful car. He would put the convertible top down as we left the schoolyard. I would wave to my classmates as they boarded the school bus. I'm sure that was a little bit of showing off on my part.

My mind was not completely on my schoolwork in those days because of John. I know I could have earned better grades. Nevertheless, God was directing my path.   John and I dated during my junior and senior years of high school and it was during my senior year that he was transferred to New York. We still wrote to each other, but his visits and letters were less frequent.

I began to spend more time doing things with my classmates: Shirley, Phoebe, and others. In February of that year (I was seventeen), my classmate Edna celebrated her birthday by having a sleepover "pajama party." She invited me along with some other classmates. Edna lived with her father and older brother, as her mother had died the previous summer. My parents gave me permission to stay overnight with her, even though my family didn't know her family. I'm still amazed at how easily I was able to get parental approval to do the things I wanted to do. It was at Edna's party where I met her brother, Claven. He was enrolled in trade school at Virginia State College, where he was studying auto mechanics. When he came home, Edna introduced Claven to her friends. I saw him with his books and began to ask him questions about his studies. Always, having had a thirst for knowledge, I wanted to know what was in his books. I recall my classmates going to bed while Claven and I continued to talk late into the night about his studies in school. I didn't know a thing about auto mechanics, but became interested just talking with him. After the slumber party, he and I had no contact for four months. During school, I would ask Edna about him from time to time, and he would send messages to me through her. I was still corresponding with John and dating him, whenever he came to Virginia.

I was one of seventy-six students who completed the requirements for graduation from Carver High School in its Class of 1960. It was at my graduation that I once again saw Claven. He was there to see his sister get her diploma. He and I spoke and he asked if he could come visit me. I didn't see any reason to say no, so my response was, "Yes." This marked the beginning of a great change in my life.

After graduation from high school and having just turned eighteen, I was at a crossroad. What did I really want to do? Would I go to college? I didn't know what I wanted to do. Mother wanted me to enroll at Virginia Union University, as Carol had upon her graduation. My desire was to travel and experience life beyond my neighborhood and Richmond. I had taken business courses in high school to prepare me for a job as a secretary. In fact, my high school yearbook lists my career goal as; wants to be a secretary. In a later chapter of this book, you will read how God made it possible for me to reach my goal, enjoy work as a secretary, and to achieve goals beyond my high school ambition.

Claven had a strong spirit of determination and quickly took center stage in my life. He did everything I asked of him, took me wherever I wanted to go and didn't mind how many of my friends came along with us. He catered to my every desire. After our first date, I was excited to spend time with him. He and I had many similarities in personality and in our lives. We both have the same birth order position as the middle child.

Claven, like me, came from a family that numbered seven. Born to William Sr. and Pannie Mae Wood, he had an older brother and sister, William Jr. and Sarah and two younger sisters, Geraldine and Edna. Claven lived near Colonial Heights, Virginia, approximately twenty miles from Bon Air. I could expect a visit from him at least once during the week and almost every Sunday.

Claven had a nice car, a 1956 black and white convertible Oldsmobile, which he kept shiny and clean. He would come to visit on Sundays, dressed to attend church with my family and me, then he would have dinner and spend the remainder of the day with us. Sometimes when he did not arrive at the house before we left for church, I'd look around in the church and he would be sitting in the back. My parents liked him, especially because he was willing to attend church with the family. I remember my father asking, "Girl, how many boyfriends are you going to have?"

Claven was very strong-willed, yet he was a gentleman. He worked at Roundtree Pontiac in Petersburg, Virginia, repairing automobiles. We dated frequently and went to many different places, such as the movies at the Booker T. and Walker theaters in Richmond, dances at Loving Union Hall and Gregory's on Hull Street, activities at Jones Lake in Chesterfield County; and concerts at Richmond's Mosque to see such singers as Jackie Wilson, Sam Cooke and other stars. We enjoyed sharing our time with each other. My high school buddies: Shirley, her sister Ruth Ella, Phoebe, and Edna often went with us to many functions. Dating Claven was fun and I continued to enjoy my teen years just having fun, (no smoking, no drinking and no sex) dancing to the music of our time, eating out and socializing with friends.

My classmates went in many directions after graduation and I kept in touch with many of them. Some of the members of Carver's Class of 1960 got married, while others had married during our senior year. Others went on to college and into the military. Shortly after Claven and I started dating, we attended the wedding of a classmate, Forrest Mae. I caught her wedding bouquet and, as the common belief goes, it was predicted I would be the next to marry. My emotions were mixed about what to do about my relationship with both John and Claven. I enjoyed the company of both of them and I was still writing to John. However, I had not seen John for quite some time. Claven was different from John because he was real serious, and seemed to want a commitment from the beginning. I began to date him without telling John simply because I didn't know how to tell him.

I often entertained my company sitting under a tree in the front yard of our house. There was a sense of privacy in the yard that couldn't be found in our small house where my parents and siblings were always close by. During the early 60's it was considered cool for a boyfriend/girlfriend to trade something with each other. One day, as Claven and I sat in the yard, I gave him my high school ring that he wore on a chain around his neck. This was a sign that we were dating steady.

That summer I took a job babysitting for a white family who lived near us. My mind was made up that I would not babysit for long, because I wanted adventure in my life. I was also dealing with "Jim Crow laws" in the South and was constantly reminded of the humiliating experiences of having to use untidy segregated public facilities, having to stand to eat while seats were available, but reserved for whites only and going through white people's back doors.

Claven's birthday came that July, just a little over one month after we started dating. He and I celebrated his 22nd birthday by going to the movies at Bellwood Drive-in, then going to eat at our favorite place, the "What-A-Burger" shop, both located on Jefferson Davis Highway. There were few, if any, restaurants in the area that served African Americans. After the celebration was over, Claven, while driving to his home in Colonial Heights, fell asleep at the wheel. He had an accident that totally destroyed his car which caused him to be without transportation. Claven no longer had transportation to visit me. Sometimes, he would borrow his father's truck, but he knew I didn't like going out in a truck, especially after riding in nice cars.

Within a month after his car accident, he totally surprised me during a visit. On a hot summer day in August, while sitting in the front yard of our home sipping ice tea, he proposed to me. His words sent a shock through me. In total dismay, I said to him, "We've only been dating for a couple of months." We had, however, spent a lot of time together and the reality was that I really liked him a lot. I told him I'd only known him for a few months and needed some time. He said, "I've had girlfriend's before I met you. I love you and want you to be my wife so that we can be together forever." I realized he was serious and it wasn't long before I decided I was in love with him and accepted his proposal. I approached my parents with the news and they immediately gave me a litany of reasons I didn't want to hear. Numerous attempts were made, but no matter how many times I tried to discuss it, they wouldn't listen to me. I must admit we were two naïve young people who didn't know much about life, let alone love and marriage. Claven and I continued to date, spending as much time as possible together. He continued to come to visit me, because

I couldn't drive nor did I have any transportation. He introduced me to his cousin, Plum Sharpe. We would double date with Plum and his girlfriend, Eva Dorothy, who later became his wife. Plum encouraged us to get married. He and Eva were also planning to marry. We found comfort knowing that we had someone who was in support of our plans. The four of us enjoyed entertainment at various places in and around Richmond. Our friendship with Plum and Eva continues to this day. On each date, Claven would talk about sex and marriage. I made my position of no sex prior to marriage clear to him, giving him the opportunity to go on his way if he so desired. He reluctantly agreed with my position and we continued to date.

At the end of August, sitting in our yard on a hot summer evening, Claven lovingly presented me with a diamond engagement ring. What a surprise this was! I did not hesitate and accepted the ring as he placed it on my finger. I was mesmerized by the whole event. He hadn't asked my ring size, instead he used my high school class ring, which I had allowed him to wear. I didn't know a thing about diamonds but I knew this was a beautiful ring, and I wanted to own it. It was my first piece of jewelry. Claven's salary was only about $40.00 per week and he told me that he had gotten the ring from a pawnshop in Petersburg, and had used his whole week's pay to buy it. I enjoyed Claven's company and was happy he had chosen me to be his wife. Claven's middle child spirit of determination had gotten me to commit to marriage, even though I'd only known him for a few months. Receiving a diamond ring at eighteen made me feel like I was on top of the world. I forgot about almost everything else, focusing entirely on marrying Claven.

More than before, I continued trying to convince Mother to agree to my getting married. I badly wanted her consent, but she continued to refuse. When I talked to my father, his words were, "You should listen to your mother." I reflected on the lovely wedding they provided my oldest sister. I knew it had cost the family a lot of money and now that it was my turn I felt I was being denied my opportunity. Furthermore, I had played a key role in Carol's wedding. I felt I was not being treated fairly by my parents. The neighbors questioned my decision. Some of them told my parents that I didn't know what I was doing, planning to marry someone that I hardly knew. Although these were the same people who had helped nurture and encourage me earlier, I began to feel upset with them because they were not providing the same support for me now. I was never a behavior problem for my parents, but was labeled as the headstrong middle child by a few people in the community.

Even though my parents liked Claven, they questioned why we were rushing to get married. My response was, "Claven wants us to be together." Claven's persistence caused me to make the decision to take control of things and find a solution to our dilemma. Claven's and my birth order, both of us being the middle child, played a key role in this situation. Together, we developed a marriage plan.

I remember people asked me about John and my future plans with him. I didn't know what to tell the neighbors and I wasn't sure how to tell John. I decided not to tell him anything about my engagement and desire to marry Claven. It wasn't until after several months of marriage that I finally wrote my last letter to John and told him the news. It was a difficult letter to write because he had meant so much to me. I can't recall exactly what I wrote in my letter to him. In his response, my last letter from him, dated April 21, 1961, he wrote, "I think about all the times we used to have. I hope you don't mind but I carry four pictures of you with me all the time...No Barbara, since you the right girl hasn't come along (smile). Oh, don't get me wrong, I go out with lots of girls but I am not serious with any...I see now it isn't every day one meets someone like you". He asked that we continue writing, but I couldn't, and our relationship ended with his letter. I was deeply touched by his response and made a decision to forever keep his letter as a reminder of our special friendship and the happiness he brought to my teen years.

PART TWO

Taking a Serious Step into an Early Marriage

Claven was twenty-two when he proposed to me that August day (1960). Our courtship lasted only four months, however it seemed like much longer because we spent so much time together. Unsuccessful at getting my parents to approve of our desire to marry, we took matters into our own hands. We'd already discussed our desire to marry with some of my friends: Nina, Phoebe, Shirley and Edna. They were all in support of our decision. Nina had eloped with Thomas when we were all seniors in high school. She and Thomas were some of our closest friends. They explained the whole process of eloping, and it sounded like the answer Claven and I needed. We planned our elopement trip, taking them up on their offer to drive us to North Carolina, where they had been married. They knew where to go and what was necessary; get a blood test, wait for the results, get a marriage license and be married before a Justice of the Peace, all in one day. The four of us were so excited about the plans.

Mother, being the wise woman that she was, suspected I was up to something, when I no longer brought up the subject of marriage with her daily. I had gone shopping with her and Gloria as usual on Saturday and I used my babysitting money to buy a new dress. I purchased an inexpensive sleeveless blue dress from Rayless, packed it and a few other items into Mother's old suitcase. I hid the suitcase under the bed until it was time for me to leave.

The plan was that Nina and Thomas would come to pick me up during the middle of the night. I went to bed in my day clothes so that I would be ready when they arrived. They were not to blow the car horn, as I would be watching for the car lights. Well, Thomas blew the horn anyway. That woke Mother, who was a light sleeper. As I got my suitcase and was about to leave through the front door, Mother approached me asking, "Where are you going?" I told her that Claven and I were going to get married and that Nina was taking us out of state. I had never seen Mother so upset. She said I didn't know what I was doing and that I should talk with my father. When she went to wake him, I ran from the house as fast as I could. I didn't want to be stopped because Claven was waiting for me. I quickly jumped in the car and off we went to Colonial Heights to pick up Claven. I clearly recall it was a rainy night in Virginia because I got soaked running to the car.

Claven was ready and waiting when we reached his home. He was just as excited as I was. Our elopement plan was working. Edna had changed her mind and decided she would not go with us. Another classmate and friend, Shirley, went along as a witness. All five of us loaded in Thomas' car and headed off to North Carolina. We laughed and talked about school days and how we had planned this day, while the torrential rain continued the entire trip of over 100 miles to Warrenton. Everything worked out just as Nina and Thomas had informed us it would. We were able to complete all of the necessary requirements and were married before a Justice of the Peace on October 8, 1960. The total cost was less than $40. It took Claven's entire week's pay to cover the expenses. I had spent all of my money for the dress and other items that I needed. Once married, Claven and I had about $3.00 between us. Though we had no money, we had each other. We laughed for years to come that we did not even have enough money left to reimburse Thomas for his expenses. Nina, Thomas, Claven and I have remained close friends over the years.

My life drastically changed after becoming a married woman. Our wedding night was spent at my father-in-law's house, that became our first home as a married couple. When we arrived at the house in late evening, it was full of people. My father-in-law and his new wife, Mrs. Ethel, were there, as was my sister-in-law Edna. Claven's other sister, Geraldine, was also there with her husband David. Everyone greeted us warmly and with congratulations. David appeared to be the happiest of all, teasing Claven about having a wife. He said, "Man, you don't know what you're in for." I couldn't tell whether David's teasing meant Claven was in for something good or something bad. Nevertheless, Claven didn't seem bothered by it, as he took my suitcase to his room. We could not afford a hotel room. We didn't receive any gifts, not even a card. From the very beginning, with the help of God, we made it on our own.

The following day, Claven and I returned to my home to show my parents our marriage license. While I was happy to be married, I felt a little sad, because I knew my parents were disappointed. I was surprised, when we told them we were married and had a license to show them, as they reluctantly accepted our actions and wished us well. However, I could see the hurt on Mother's face. I knew they thought the marriage would not last because we were so young and we hadn't known each other very long. Mother knew from her own struggles the difficulties I could face. I'm sure she wanted better for me. My neighbors couldn't believe what I had done. I was the talk of the neighborhood, especially among the women, because I ran away to get married.

Our married life started with no money and very little life experience. Claven's salary now was approximately $50.00 a week. We were living with my father-in-law and his wife. She made sure that we paid for our own food, the household items that we used and that we contributed to the utilities and anything else she felt necessary. My father-in-law, a very quiet gentleman, allowed his wife to handle the affairs of the house. Edna, my sister-in-law, who also lived with us, was employed and therefore she was also required to pay a share of the household expenses. My father-in-law, a deacon at Mt. Pleasant Baptist Church in Chesterfield County, did all he could to keep peace in his home and make life good for us all. In spite of his humble efforts, there was a lot of discord between his wife and his children. I often thought about how this living situation sometimes made me feel like I was in the middle. I was caught between the stepmother and the stepchildren. I tried my best to get along with everyone. Claven, Edna and I continued to spend a lot of time socializing together. I also became close with his sisters Sarah, Geraldine.

Claven and I visited my parents almost every weekend. We continued to attend church, sometimes with my family. We also continued to go to dances and other social events with my classmates from Carver. We enjoyed life as a couple. Claven always worked hard and saved as much money as we could. After about six months of living in his father's house we decided to move. By this time, Claven had fully acquired auto body repair skills. He decided to seek employment in this field in the Washington, D.C. area. We packed up one day and he took me to Richmond to stay with my oldest sister, and then he was off to Washington. In a matter of days he found a job and a rooming house where we could live. He returned to my sister's house for me right away. With only the clothes we owned and a few small household items we drove our 1955 Ford to our new home.

Claven and I arrived in Washington in early April 1961. Our rooming house was located at 16th and V Streets, Northwest. I really felt strange, being away from my family and familiar surroundings. During our first three weeks in Washington I went to work with Claven every day. To this day we still disagree about the reason I did this. Claven said that I was afraid to stay home without him, but I knew he was afraid for me to stay home alone. Our landlord asked if I had a job, because I dressed and left the house daily. When I told her, "No", she asked why I went to work with Claven everyday. Neither of us could answer the question. It has since become a family joke in our house and even our sons now laugh about it.

Claven and I continued enjoying our lives together. We didn't know anyone in the area, so we spent all of our time together. I prepared our dinners, after we ate we would walk up 16th Street to Meridian Hill Park. We would sit in the park until dusk talking about our future plans. On one of our visits to the park, Claven took a knife from his pocket and carefully crafted a heart in a large tree. Then he carved our initials inside it and said our love should last forever. I was moved to tears by his actions. For many years after that, we would go back to the park to look at the carving in the tree.

Our social life was going to church service on Sundays at Isle of Patmos Baptist Church, which was located at 15th & U Streets, N.W. The owner of the rooming house, Geneva, would tease Claven and I, claiming that we stayed in bed most of the time. The other people rooming in the house were much older than we were, and their lifestyles were very different. They hosted parties on the weekends, drank alcohol and did a lot of cursing, using language I had never heard before. We avoided interaction with them as much as we could. One day, out of the clear blue, Geneva asked me if I was pregnant. I responded with a quick "No." She replied, "I've been watching the way you walk lately and your complexion has that look." I wasn't feeling any different than usual and still had my menses. I possibly had gained a pound or two, but paid little attention to it. She said I should go see a doctor. We didn't know any, nor had we thought about finding a doctor in the area. So, Geneva gave me the name of her doctor. The next day I contacted, Dr. Oliver, a family physician, with an office located on 11th and T Streets, Northwest, which was in the basement of a large house. He examined me and told me that Geneva's diagnosis was correct. I was indeed three months pregnant. Dr. Oliver referred me to Georgetown University Hospital for further examination and testing. What a shock this was for us. We had not given any thought to having a baby.

Claven was extremely happy when I told him the news. I was happy, yet apprehensive. I really had not adjusted to living in Washington yet and was already beginning to feel homesick. And now, I was about to have a baby. After the shock wore off, I was afraid. I began to get sick with worry. I didn't know what to do with a baby. Claven knew I was frightened about living far from home and being pregnant. He became very attentive to my needs and was truly a happy father-in-waiting. He would constantly call home to check on me during his work break. And like clockwork, he would promptly arrive home at the end of his workday. We continued to take our daily stroll from V Street, Northwest, up 16th Street to Meridian Hill Park. Claven decided that, with a baby on the way, we should find another place to live. Still, we couldn't afford an apartment so he found another rooming house at 1243 Eye Streets, Northeast. We lived with a Christian woman named Mrs. Eleanor Hill and her daughter. We experienced a very pleasant, family atmosphere living in her home.

At home all day, bored and pregnant, I enrolled in Atlantic Business College to further my education. A high school classmate, Mary Rollings, and her husband, Joseph, had also recently moved to Washington. Mary contacted us and she and I resumed our friendship formed at Carver High. We did a lot of socializing together. Mary also enrolled in Atlantic Business College and she and I took all of our classes together. We would catch the bus to school and Claven would come to pick us up after class. Not being very familiar with Washington, we would sometimes get lost and it would take hours to reach our final destination. Mary and I graduated high school and business college together. Later, she and I started our federal government careers together, after taking the Civil Service test at the Old Post Office Building.

I received prenatal care through the clinic at Georgetown University Hospital. While attending the clinic, I met another expectant mother whose name was also, Barbara. She and I shared our experiences and our families became friends.

Claven and I celebrated our first wedding anniversary, October 1961, by just being together. Our baby was due within a few days, so we were anxiously awaiting the arrival. We spent the night talking about plans for our future. Claven's income had increased, but still we were living in one room. Just about two weeks after our anniversary, I gave birth to our first child on October 17, 1961.

Our blessing was a precious little boy. Claven became a proud father who adored our child. The moment we looked at our son together, at Georgetown University Hospital, Claven and I felt a true connection in a way that words cannot describe. When the subject of a name for our child arose, Claven immediately said, "His name will be the same as mine." The discussion ended and we named our firstborn son, Claven Jr. We took to calling him "Junior" right away. Neither Claven nor I had any experience caring for an infant. Along with the joys of parenthood we had our fears and worries. It was at this point that I knew I needed my mother. Right away I contacted Mother for help.

She came to visit us and helped us with the baby. By now, Mother had two grandchildren already, my niece Carol (named after her mother) and my oldest brother's daughter, Brenda. Our son was her third grandchild. Mrs. Hill, the owner of the rooming house, also helped us care for our baby. When our son was born, we did not have a bed for him. We removed a drawer from our used dresser to make this his bed. We later purchased a crib from the Salvation Army on H Street, N.E. Claven continued to work hard and we saved our money. A short time later, we moved out of the rooming house and into our own apartment on 10th and D Streets Northeast.

I soon started to work for the government. By this time, my brother James (Jimmy) and his wife Gladys had relocated to Washington. While Gladys had her own baby girl, Brenda, she became Claven Jr.'s first babysitter. Every other weekend, Claven and I would pack up our baby and make the two hour trip to Richmond and Colonial Heights to visit relatives. I had not learned how to drive yet, so Claven did all of the driving. On occasion, Mary and Joseph would ride to Richmond with us to visit Mary's family. We were enjoying parenthood, and things were improving for us financially. When I decided I needed to learn how to drive, Claven taught me by taking me to the D.C. Stadium parking lot on Saturdays and Sundays to practice. After a few driving lessons, I was ready to take the test and get my driving license. I passed the test on the first try, even though I failed the parking portion. I really enjoyed the freedom of being able to go places without depending on Claven or having to use public transportation.

Claven purchased my first car, a 1963 Falcon, blue with a white convertible top. The vehicle had been wrecked and was considered damaged beyond repair. His excellent skills in auto collision repair allowed him to completely rebuild the car within a few months. He repainted it and the car, my new toy, was almost like new. I loved driving around D. C. with the top down. We didn't have seat belts and babies weren't required to ride in car seats back then. I placed my baby boy on the seat beside me as I drove around the city. I was able to drive the car to my first job at National Institutes of Health (NIH), in Bethesda, Maryland. Claven was also working in Bethesda at Tony's Auto Body, so we rode to work together. Our income increased, now that we were both working. And, in September 1962, we purchased our first home in Northeast for $12,500.

The house had six rooms and one bath. It was a two-floor row house with three bedrooms upstairs and fireplace in the living room. It was sufficient to meet our needs.

About one month after I started my job, I found myself pregnant for the second time. I continued my employment as a medical records clerk until one month before the birth of our second child. Knowing I would need help, I persuaded my mother to come and stay with us for a while. My parents and my sister, Gloria, would come and stay with us on weekends. On June 16th, 1963, Father's Day, God blessed us with another little boy. I clearly recall the events of that day. Calvin was born, after I ate a big Sunday dinner, celebrating Father's Day with my husband. I went into labor and was rushed from our home in Northeast to Georgetown University Hospital. Shortly thereafter, our second son was born. Claven was again overjoyed at the birth of another son. I said to him, "This child is your lifetime Father's Day gift." The naming of our child was important and I decided to give him a name as close to his father's name as possible. That is why we chose Calvin. Claven and I agreed that our sons would both have the same initials, C.A.W.

Immediately after Calvin's birth, we were told he was sick. His skin pigment was very yellow and he had developed jaundice. We began to wonder if our baby would survive. The doctors informed us he needed an immediate blood transfusion. They told us something about our blood types not matching and that this was what caused the problem. We began to blame each other. I was only twenty-one and Claven was twenty-four. We had not heard of such a condition before. Being inexperienced, we didn't question the doctors' recommendation, and granted permission for the procedure.

I now know God was there in the midst of it all. At the end of my three-day hospital stay, I had to leave our baby behind and this was a very difficult thing for me to do. We visited him daily to check on his progress. After about a week, we brought him home. He had numerous tiny needle holes in his arms, hands and feet from the transfusions. Claven and I prayed during this time that God would take care of our son. Our prayers were answered.

We loved our sons and were very attentive to their needs. Mother was in constant contact with me. She provided as much help as she could from a distance. By now, all of my siblings, except Gloria, had left home and were living on their own. My parents soon relocated to Washington, D.C. and right away the family found a church and continued their lifestyle of serving God. Gloria enrolled at Eastern High School, where she graduated with the Class of 1966. It was a real comfort to have Mother close by.

In addition to being a mother and a wife, I had an interest in civic and community affairs. The year 1963 was a special time for me for two reasons. First, there was the birth of our second son, Calvin. Second was my opportunity to participate in one of the most significant events of the Civil Rights Movement, the March on Washington, which was held August 28, 1963. I recall my early years of growing up in the segregated South, when I read about the work of Dr. Martin Luther King, Jr. and the Civil Rights Movement. Once I learned of the March on Washington, I enthusiastically decided to participate in the demonstration with Dr. King and others. Both my husband and mother felt I should not participate because Calvin was only two months old. As long as I was certain both of my sons would be taken care of, I was going to be a part of this major event. I wanted to personally see and hear Dr. King because I greatly admired him. I discussed my plans with my classmate, Mary, and her husband, Joseph, as well as with co-workers and other friends. Mary, then seven months pregnant with her first child, decided not to attend. Claven also decided not to participate. However, Joseph and I, along with some work colleagues, met at our house and together we walked downtown to the Mall and the Lincoln Memorial. We joined over two hundred thousand people who had come from all across the Nation for this symbolic march. When we reached the Mall, the sight of so many people lifted our spirits. We saw a mix of people; African Americans, Whites and others, who had traveled by plane, train, bus, cars, or on foot, like us to the March. This exciting and moving experience left an indelible mark on me. I felt privileged to personally hear Dr. King deliver his famous "I Have A Dream" speech. I felt a sense of enthusiasm as I thought about the oppressive Jim Crow laws of my childhood and the unfair experiences of having to use separate public facilities in Richmond. And now, I was standing among Whites that were in support of equality for all. I was truly amazed and inspired with hope for a more equal future for my people.

As I reflect back over nearly four decades, my serious step into an early marriage, I have mixed emotions; joy and happiness, sadness and disappointments. Both Claven's and my middle child personalities of constantly being determined to have our way led to some fussing and fighting, and a brief period of separation. Sometimes, I felt as though I was on a swing going high and low as I observed Claven's pull away the family to spend time drinking and hanging out with his buddies. We were so close as marriage partners and parents, I couldn't believe what was happening. We overcame our marital problems, reunited and tried our best to make the marriage work. The sum of the this chapter of my life is that joy and happiness far outweigh the sorrow and regrets.

Rearing Our Sons

I took my responsibilities as a parent very seriously and provided love and care for our sons as best I could. I taught my children many of the same values that my parents and others taught me. Our sons were blessed and received nurturing from a number of other people who greatly influenced their lives. They had the love of their maternal grandparents who were always available to lend a helping hand. Their paternal grandfather, aunts, uncles, other relatives, neighbors and friends (who were like family), also provided them guidance and direction when they were growing up. My mother was their only babysitter for quite some time, until she took a job.

Claven Jr. and Calvin, only eighteen months apart, benefited and bonded as a result of their close ages. While they weren't twins, I often treated them as though they were. I'm certain that my actions had both advantages and possibly some disadvantages. I remember being excited to dress them alike to have their pictures taken. As they grew up, even to this day, I haven't noticed competition between them. I believe they've shared a very close relationship from birth.

As a young mother, working outside of the home, the responsibility of caring for two small children was often a struggle. In the early 1960's I was not aware of disposable diapers so I used cloth diapers. This meant that I emptied and washed a lot of diapers since both children wore them at the same time. I remember the relief I felt when the diaper period ended. My sons drank canned Carnation milk mixed with boiled water not Similac, Enfamil, or other ready-made formulas that are used today. I used glass bottles for milk and juice, which after each use had to be washed and sterilized. This was a major daily task. I'm not aware of anyone in this generation sterilizing bottles, instead they are using mostly plastic or disposable bottles. Both sons wore braided hair before it became the fashionable style. Tucked away in my treasure chest now are their braids, I saved from their first haircuts when they were each about one year old. Their braids and a few pieces of clothing became keepsakes.

Our sons began their formal education in the D.C. Public School System, attending Maury Elementary School on Constitution Avenue, N.E. I recall walking each of them to school on their first day. Even though I worked outside of the home, I made sure most of my non-working hours were spent with our sons, caring for them and providing them guidance for life. Our sons were happy little guys who enjoyed life at the level we could afford to them. Our combined incomes provided a decent quality of life for our family. The bed was no longer a dresser drawer; we were able to purchase bunk beds. Claven worked long hours, especially after he established his own business in 1964. Many evenings after I had completed my workday at the office, I'd pick up my two young sons and we'd spend the evening at the business. While they played, I assisted my husband by taking care of the paperwork.

By 1968 my classmate and sister-in-law, Edna, had married a wonderful man named Alexander (Alex). Edna, Alex and their son, Mark, joined us on family outings and vacations. Mark was a good playmate for our sons. Alex, a fisherman at heart, organized many all day fishing trips for the family. We enjoyed many meals of fresh fish caught during these fishing outings. Each summer we looked forward to our family vacation in Atlantic City. During the late1960's and 1970's, Atlantic City was a popular family vacation spot. There were no gambling casinos and we rented an efficiency apartments, right on the boardwalk for a very reasonable cost. We took along food from home, cooked and ate in the apartment. During the early mornings, we rented and rode bicycles up and down the boardwalk, enjoying the morning breeze.

Nina and Thomas also moved to Washington in the late 1960's and continued to be among our closest friends. Their children, Shirley, Thomas Jr., and Cathy, and our sons practically grew up together, almost as one family. Nina worked close to home and looked out for the neighborhood children. Whenever our sons behaved in a manner that she thought was inappropriate and would displease us, she would not hesitate to correct them and to inform me. For this, I'm so thankful. The boys did many mischievous things and received appropriate punishment. Once they took their BB gun outside and chased the other kids. They also shot a hole in the center of our television set. These boys were boys indeed. They were latchkey children during their early adolescence years. However, Nina was just a few doors away and provided any assistance they needed.

In 1972, while the boys were still in elementary school, we moved to Glenarden, Maryland. This was a small community located about fourteen miles east of Washington. Ironically, our sons' experiences growing up in Glenarden were somewhat similar to my childhood experiences in Bon Air. The community was then and still is approximately ninety-nine percent African American. The neighbors in the community watched out for each other, especially the children, and provided help as needed.

Our sons attended Glenarden Elementary School, until the Prince George's County schools were integrated in 1973. After busing took place, the children attended James McHenry Elementary School in Lanham, where I was a very active parent with the PTA. After completing elementary school, our sons were bused to Martin Luther King Jr. Middle School in Beltsville. Claven, Jr. and Calvin were athletes, participating in soccer, basketball and wrestling during their junior high school days. I didn't know everything that was going on in their lives, but I tried to keep up with their activities. I knew our children were influenced by their peers. I felt safe knowing that our sons associated with children in the neighborhood of Glenarden. As a result, there were no major negative peer influences from their friends. I reared them with an old fashioned style, "Do as I say without asking any questions," and they did most of the time.

My husband worked long hours to manage the business and was not able to attend many of their school functions. Nevertheless, I made sure that I was there to support them. Fortunately for me I had a supervisor who was very supportive of family and allowed me as much time off as possible. Many days, I would leave my job in Washington, D.C., taking my lunchtime to meet with a teacher or to see the boys participate in a school event. As I walked down the hallways of Martin Luther King, Jr. Middle School I would hear students say, "There goes Jr. and Calvin's mother...she's always here."

Our sons experienced two vastly different cultures growing up. One of living in a community where people lived decent lives caring for one another and the other, a culture of a drug-infested section of Northwest Washington where the family business was located (14th and Church Street, Northwest). I believe many factors played a role in their avoiding destructive behaviors. The main reason was their experience of life in a caring family and community.

My husband and I frequently took in family members who were in need of help, as most African American families did from time to time. We shared our home with many relatives, enabling our sons to further connect with extended family members. One or two of the relatives had at one time used illegal drugs. Our sons were aware of this, and it was a topic of discussion in our home to prevent them from such behavior. In Northwest Washington, the boys saw everything from intoxicated men and women on the streets to drug addicts and prostitutes. They informed me of the heroin needles they saw on the streets as they walked to and from the auto paint store to get supplies for the business. The boys were involved in sports and were conscious of staying healthy in order to participate. My husband, Claven, a boxing fan, encouraged their interest in this sport. Both Claven Jr. and Calvin watched Sugar Ray Leonard win the Gold Medal in boxing in 1976. After this experience, and the strong encouragement from their father, they developed an interest in boxing. As teenagers, from 1976 through 1979, they participated in boxing in the communities of Glenarden and Palmer Park, Maryland. To their honor, they received numerous trophies as Champion and Runner-up during this period. Sugar Ray Leonard served as referee for one of the boxing events. I was a proud mother witnessing my sons' achievements in this area.

Both sons went through their middle school years often being mistaken for one another by some of their teachers and other people as well. By this time, I had stopped dressing them alike. Calvin followed Claven Jr. in most activities. I did not have to deal with rivalry between them, as they were close. Claven Jr. watched out for his younger brother and they were protective of each other. Both my husband and I were strong disciplinarians and we balanced each other in rearing our sons. We matured enough to suppress our strong-willed middle child personalities in order to work together to rear our children. Our sons were taught the love of Christ and were required to attend church and participate in church-related activities. The boys were baptized at Bibleway Church pastored by the late Bishop Smallwood Williams. But, for the most part, they received spiritual guidance at the Fisherman of Men Church pastored by Bishop Clarence Groover and Praise Temple Church pastored by their uncle, Elder James Quarels.

After completing Middle School, both sons attended Bladensburg Senior High School, Bladensburg, Maryland, where they graduated in 1979 and 1981. During their high school years I continued my frequent visits to the school to show them support and monitor their progress as closely as possible. Both sons started driving when they were about sixteen and it was a big help to me to send them on errands. However, they had a curfew and most of the time they obeyed it. I set rules and enforced them just as mother had done when I was growing up. They conspired and kept things from me because they felt I was too strict. I recall one Friday night Calvin drove Claven Jr. to a young lady's house in Southern Maryland. The plan was to have her relative bring Claven home. At 4:00 a.m. I woke up to find that my son was not in the house. I panicked, woke my husband and Calvin, then I insisted that Calvin drive us to the young lady's house. We arrived at the house close to 5:00 a.m. finding several cars in the yard, a house full of people laughing, talking and seemingly unaware of the hour. I rushed in to find my son among the crowd. The expression on the faces of Claven friends was shock. I'm certain they thought I was insane to drag our whole family to this party in the middle of the night. The young lady explained she could not get anyone to drive Claven Jr. home, and the party had continued through the night. I didn't want to hear any excuses. Needless to say, his relationship with this young lady didn't last long. This experience taught both sons to obey the curfew rule in our house.

When Claven Jr. was in his senior year, he was faced with a problem. His English teacher was unfair in how she treated him, especially in assigning grades. I met with her on several occasions, and she insisted that Claven would not participate in the class. I questioned Claven and found the opposite to be true. After several unsuccessful discussions with the teacher, the counselor and Bladensburg's Principal, James Foran, I was forced to take matters into my own hands. I went to the officials of the Prince George's County School Board asking for their intervention. Within a short period of time, a representative was sent to the school. He observed Claven Jr. in class, checked his work and grades, and spoke with the teacher. I received a letter from the School Board stating that my concerns were valid and the problem had been resolved. Later, our son's close friends would jokingly say to each other, "If you have a problem with a teacher, get Mrs. Wood...she can work it out."

Calvin progressed through high school well until his senior year. He played around in class, talking too much with the young ladies and fell behind in his studies. I applied tough love and enrolled him in two high schools at the same time — Bladensburg by day and Largo by night so he could graduate on time. Thank God, he ended up with a fairly respectable grade point average and graduated with his class.

Upon completion of high school, Claven Jr., like me, became a public servant. He enrolled in Prince George's Community College where he earned his Degree in Electronic Technology. He had been employed, during his summers in high school, as a Security Aide with the Smithsonian Institution, Air and Space Museum. He has continued his employment as a career employee with the agency in his chosen field. I am proud of his accomplishments and honored that he chose to follow my path to become a public servant.

Calvin, upon his high school graduation, decided to follow his father into the family business. I am proud of the reputation that Calvin has established with the customers. They speak highly of his integrity in business. I am blessed with two wonderful sons for whom I am thankful to God. I know I may have made some mistakes along the way, but I did the best I knew how in raising them. For all that they are, I give God glory for His guidance, my husband and my parents for their unwavering love and support.

Becoming A Godmother

In 1974, while working at the United States Department of Transportation in Washington, I met and befriended a woman named Jeanette Palmer (deceased). This was the beginning of a new and wonderful chapter in my life, even though neither of us knew it at the time. Jeanette was an extremely warm and friendly person, she and I often had lunch together. We discovered we lived near each other and, as a result, established a carpool. Jeanette was the mother of three young children: Tammi, LaTanya and Duane. Our families became friends, frequently visiting each other and attending each other's family events. I admired her beautiful little girls, especially because I didn't have a daughter of my own. Tammi was the oldest of the three children, born a little more than two years before Jeanette met and married her husband.

When I met Jeanette I was a member of Praise Temple Church, Washington, D.C. where my brother-in-law, James Quarles, served as the pastor. I invited Jeanette and her family to attend church with me. She happily accepted and our friendship grew even closer. She and I spent many hours sharing the rain and sunshine of our lives. Early in our friendship Jeanette told me she admired my relationship with my family and was inspired by my spiritual values. She asked me if I would consider being Tammi's godmother. I was so surprised by her request I didn't know how to answer her question. I asked, "Are you sure you want me to be her godmother and why?" Jeanette explained that she wanted someone who would be like a second mother for her daughter. She believed that I could provide advice and guidance beyond what she was capable of doing. She was adamant about having someone in Tammi's life to care for her in case she no longer could do so. She said, "I've observed you with your children, and I want Tammi to have the same love and discipline." I felt deeply honored and touched by her words. It brought me happiness to tell her yes. Tammi was a beautiful little girl and I felt as though I had been given a special gift. What I didn't know at that time, Jeanette was seriously ill with multiple sclerosis.

Becoming Tammi's godmother created a unique relationship between our two families. I remember back in 1974 when she was a fifth grader at Bladensburg Elementary School, it was Honors Day and she was happy to see me in the audience as her support. She knew her mother could not attend the program. Each time her name was called to receive an award; perfect attendance, straight A's, safety patrol and others, I could see the excitement on her face as she looked out into the audience to make sure I was observing. I felt blessed to be able to share my time and give support to a young impressionable mind. Years later she said to me, " Your support at the Honors' Program made such a difference in my life that I made a vow to continue to do my best in school because I knew that someone cared."

I gave Tammi her first watch, a Timex with a brown leather band, when she was in elementary school. She said, "It made me feel so special." During visits to Tammi's school I talked with teachers who praised her for outstanding achievements, especially in academics. I was proud I played a part in motivating her thirst for knowledge. Jeanette could not always be at her school functions but she knew she could count on me being there.

Tammi spent a lot of time in our home and really became part of our family. To me, she was the daughter I never had. She was always a delightful child, although sometimes a little shy. I showed her the same love I showed my sons. On Sunday she would attend church with us and have dinner with our family. Tammi was fascinated with the Order of Service and soon became a part of our church family at Praise Temple. I don't recall if I ever actually asked her if she wanted to sing in the children's choir; I just signed her up. She was always obedient and did as she was told. She later told me how scared she was to be standing in front of people she didn't know trying to sing. She loved books and sports, not singing. Her spiritual growth came early in her life, and she accepted Christ as her Savior during a Sunday school service at the age of seven.

She had a special quality about her, even as a child, keenly observing her surroundings. Whenever she was in our home, she was an excellent little helper and looked for things to do. My sons would expect her to clean up their untidy rooms. On some holidays Tammi would spend time with us as well as with her own family. Our sons looked out for her as though she was their little sister.

When Tammi was in high school her family moved from Maryland to Dothan, Alabama and she enrolled in Northview High School. Emotionally, I felt a deep loss when she and her family relocated. The miles were overcome by phone calls, letters and cards. She would write often and inform me of her school activities. She also visited when she could. I recall a special Thanksgiving, when Tammi was about fourteen and traveled from Alabama to spend the holiday with us. This was one of

69

my happiest Thanksgivings, because it felt as though I had my three children with me. She and I would sit up late into the night, drinking hot chocolate, our favorite late night drink, and talking about life. During these times that I provided her with guidance, leadership and advice on life's challenges. Throughout her teenage years we continued to build upon the foundation we'd started early in her life. We shared peaceful moments that included laughter and uplifting conversations, as well as the painful times during her mother's illness and later when Jeanette died at the age of forty-six.

Tammi continued to excel in school and graduated with honors from Northview, receiving a four-year Presidential Scholarship to Alabama State University in Montgomery, Alabama. While matriculating through Alabama State University (ASU), she became Miss Alabama State 1989/ 90. This brought excitement to all of us who were involved in her life. As an ASU student, she enjoyed working in the Office of Communications and Public Affairs, where John Knight, Jr. was, and still is the Director. I recall one occasion when my family traveled to California to join Tammi and her family. She was competing in the Miss African American Pageant representing Alabama State University as Miss ASU. We were so proud of her. Also, we traveled to Montgomery, Alabama, our first visit to the birthplace of the civil rights movement, to witness her graduation with honors from Alabama State.

Tammi continued her education, earning a Master's Degree in marketing from the University of Baltimore, where she again graduated with honors. It has been and continues to be a joy sharing Tammi's life as her godmother. Her glowing personality, spirit of love and care, as well as her dedication to self and others makes her a rare jewel. I thank God for Tammi and for Jeanette choosing me to be her godmother.

Being A Grandparent

What surprising good news it is when you hear you are going to be a grandparent! How wonderful it is to know that your family tree is growing! Some of my greatest pleasures have been and continue to be nurturing my grandchildren.

My son, Calvin, and Christine blessed me first with the birth of my only grandson, Calvin Jr. (called Lil Calvin) on December 18, 1983. He brought about a special family closeness. I recall thinking to myself, "What a beautiful child he is!" He weighed in at six pounds, ten ounces. Upon first laying eyes on him, I immediately saw that he had inherited features from his father and his paternal grandfather. His skin, eye color and the shape of his eyes were all features of his paternal side of the family. He looked almost exactly like his father did at birth. I also noticed something else I had seen some twenty years earlier. I observed the same joy and admiration on my son's face upon the birth of his son (Lil Calvin), that his father (Claven) had expressed at the time of his birth. There was a surge of love for this child from both maternal and paternal grandparents, as well as his five uncles, Claven Jr., Jerome, Richard Jr., Stanley and William (Bill). Once again happiness as a grandparent came for me with the birth of my second grandchild, Carmela, (Lil Calvin's sister), on March 19, 1989. She weighed in at seven pounds, two ounces.

Lil Calvin was the first grandchild on both sides of the family. His birth marked the beginning of competition between his maternal grandparents, Richard and Rebecca Proctor, and us, his paternal grandparents. Six years later, Carmela's birth added to the competition between the two sets of grandparents. I remember many of my weekend plans being canceled because the maternal grandparents had already made weekend plans which included the grandchildren. My grandchildren enjoyed all of the spoils from both sets of grandparents. However, the parents, Calvin and Christine, kept us all in line by insisting that we share the children. So we lovingly learned how to share our grandchildren and respected each other's time spent with them.

The grandchildren visited almost every other weekend and I enjoyed shopping for their clothing and food and kept the house stocked when they visited us. Everything they needed was waiting for their arrival. Enfamil, their formula, was what I used, unlike their father's formula, which was made from Carnation milk. I no longer had to sterilized bottles, as I had done twenty years earlier with my sons, because we used plastic bottles. Disposable diapers were a welcome change. On occasion I would use the blankets I had saved from when my sons were babies. Bedtime at our house took me back twenty years when our sons would be nestled in bed between my husband and me. Now, the grandchildren are practicing the same bedtime routine of crawling in bed with us to sleep. Lil Calvin and Carmela enjoyed the limelight as the only grandchildren until their sister Catarina was born on December 7, 1998. She weighed in at seven pounds and four ounces. Catarina, a bright eyed, beautiful little girl, captured the love of the entire family.

My grandchildren have been an integral part of my life. I have included them on business trips and yearly vacations. The two older grandchildren traveled with me on business trips so frequently that some of my co-workers, expecting to see them, would question their whereabouts if they weren't with me. One memorable event was when my friend and co-worker at the Justice Department, Violet, met Carmela on a trip. We spent a considerable amount of time together, shopping and dining. Violet commented, "Your granddaughter has really impressed me with her manners, confidence and maturity. I'll never forget her."

During the quality time that I spent with my grandchildren, I taught them spiritual values and I lovingly disciplined them. In an interview for this book, my grandson shared the following event: He said, "One day when I was about four years old, you gave me a beating on my legs with a belt, because I was spitting at my great grandparents (my parents). It made me realize I had done something very wrong. I never forgot it and I never did that again." I replied, "It's twelve years later and you say you still remember? Do you think I did the right thing?" He responded: "Yes, Grandmother, if I were the adult, I would have done the same thing." Lil Calvin, Carmela and Catarina are my blessings. Carmela, an honor student, is the middle grandchild and her personality reflects the characteristics of a middle child, especially that as peacemaker.

It is my belief every child is sanctified in God's sight and grandparents have a dutiful responsibility to them. I'm reminded of how my parents showed their love for our sons and all of their grandchildren. They touched and influenced the lives of their grandchildren in so many positive ways, and I'm trying to follow their example. As the family tree grows with grandchildren, so grows my responsibility as a grandparent. My treasure in life, without a doubt, is my family.

Part Three

Career
In The Federal Government

Memories of my career in the federal government (which spanned over thirty years) are numerous. I progressed to a senior level manager before retiring, received numerous accolades, and was admired by most of my co-workers for my character and work ethic. Overall, my journey through the federal government was pleasant and rewarding; however, I did experience a few incidents of racial bias and subtle sexual harassment. Occasionally, I was referred to as uppity, perhaps because of my demeanor, and once a co-worker left a message on an answering machine calling me a "n.....".

I entered federal service in August 1962 as a GS-02 Transcribing Clerk with the Department of Health, Education and Welfare, National Institutes of Health (NIH) in Bethesda, Maryland, at a yearly salary of about $2,000. I had little to no work experience, but a certificate in secretarial studies from Atlantic Business College. I was excited and anxious about starting work in the federal government. It was my first real job. I knew that I had to learn about the job and how to interact with the people, especially my supervisor who was a white female. Being from the segregated South, where I had little interaction with white people, I was apprehensive about the racial differences. I also knew I was outspoken and my personality was one of strong will. Hired as a clerk typist, I sat at a typewriter (without a correctable ribbon), along side many other clerk typists in a large room referred to as the typing pool. As I recall, fifteen women of various ages were in the typing pool and about half of the group was Afro-Americans the other half was white. We were responsible for transcribing the medical records of patients as dictated onto discs by NIH physicians. The supervisor of the pool was a middle-aged white woman named Mrs. Cavanaugh. She was a kind and courteous family woman who treated everyone as equals. The work environment was one of harmony in spite of our racial differences. I enjoyed the job and interacted well with most of the women. Everyday I arrived at work, on time, to contribute to completing the work of the office pool. I used the medical dictionary and other resources to check the correct spelling of medical terms, taking pride in doing the best I could. I looked forward to the paycheck I received at two-week intervals. After a little less than a year on the job, I left on maternity leave. For six weeks, I stayed home to care for my baby, after which I returned to my job. Shortly thereafter, I transferred to the District of Columbia government, Motor Vehicle Administration (MVA), to work as a clerk. This job was closer to my home and I received my first promotion to GS-3.

One of my duties at the MVA was to receive, via telephone, change of address requests from District of Columbia residents holding valid driver's licenses. I enjoyed this part of the job because it allowed me to talk to a lot of people. Again, I was blessed to have a kind supervisor, Gene Alber, who I felt respected his employees. I received calls from many people; some friendly, some not so friendly. I recall sitting at my desk one day when I received a call from my high school classmate,

Carolyn, who was calling to change her address and that of her husband's. When I heard her name, I began to think, "Could this be my high school classmate?" Curiosity made me ask her if she had attended Carver High School in Chester, Virginia. Her response was, "Yes." We had not talked since our high school graduation and were elated to reconnect.

During my early years as a public servant, I transferred jobs many times, usually seeking career advancement. I transferred jobs between the United States Information Agency, Veterans Administration, Smithsonian Institution and the Department of Defense. It was my first position at NIH that gave me the confidence I needed to succeed in the government. I faced challenges in several positions but prevailed nevertheless.

In 1969, I worked as a secretary at the Smithsonian Institution for the Director of Security, Colonel Grimsley. I remember the interview as if it were yesterday. Colonel Grimsley interrogated me for over an hour asking about my skills, my personality, my family and the like. Looking directly at me, he said, "I am difficult to work for and I expect nothing less than excellence from my secretary." I was already sure that I could perform the task, but he made me nervous. For this experience, I am extremely grateful, because it led to a lasting friendship. Colonel Grimsley instructed me to contact his previous secretary, Constance (Connie) Lykes, who had left the job due to her pregnancy. I followed his direction and contacted her. She told me he was a kind man, but he'll test you and she said, "He can be difficult to satisfy as a supervisor." She shared some of her experiences working for the Colonel. I appreciated her honesty.

I took on the challenge and accepted the job. Connie's words proved true. The Colonel and I had many disagreements. I did my job in a satisfactory manner, although my performance didn't always please Colonel Grimsley. He said to me on many occasions, "You should have been a Philadelphia lawyer...you're always defending yourself." I knew how to give and take and I had to practice this often working with the Colonel. I found myself taking his criticisms more frequently than I liked. Many mornings, I'd walk in the office and say, "Good morning." His response would be, "What's good about it?" Other days, he would simply say, "Keep the rest of the day good and everything will be all right." I tried my best to perform my duties and to satisfy Colonel Grimsley. I reverted back to my youthful days, when I couldn't satisfy my mother with the household chores no matter how hard I tried. So, my attitude was to do my best and forget the rest. It got to be somewhat amusing, working for Colonel Grimsley but I couldn't take it for long. I moved on within a short period of time to another job. Connie kept in touch with me to see how I managed in the job. She and her husband William (Bill) relocated back to Akron, Ohio; the friendship we established continued to flourish. Over the years, she shared information about the birth of her daughters, Kellie and Kasey. We also shared our life experiences as wives, mothers, and today we share our experiences as grandmothers, enjoying our grandchildren.

My career progressed and God continued to bless my life. In 1972, I began working as a secretary with the Department of Transportation (DOT), Federal Aviation Administration (FAA). Both my interpersonal skills and secretarial skills improved in this position and I was provided many training opportunities necessary for advancement. My social life was enhanced and some co-workers became my friends. We often played softball together on the Mall after work. During my employment with

FAA, I also met and befriended several of the original Tuskegee Airmen. These individuals were retired military personnel who worked for the FAA. Spann Watson, an original Tuskegee Airman, whose military career included a stint with the 99th Fighter Squadron during World War II, became a close friend. A true advocate for African Americans, he diligently worked to help people with career advancement issues. Spann was the kind of individual who, upon meeting you and liking you, makes you his lifetime friend. Our friendship has continued nearly thirty years and remains strong.

In 1975, I transferred from the FAA to the headquarters Department of Transportation (DOT), Office of the Secretary. I enjoyed this job and had a great supervisor, Michael Finkelstein, who was a kind-hearted family man and was very supportive of his employees. I did my work and developed a wonderful working relationship with Mike. He approved all of my time off when I wanted to attend my sons' daytime school functions. Mike's philosophy was that as long as the work was completed, his employees could take time off. Mike was the kind of person, who treated all of his employees fairly and he included support staff in all aspects of the job whenever possible.

I recall my secretarial work with Mike and others on the Washington Metro-rail System project, and he made the decision to give the secretaries the opportunity to go on the first test ride of the Metro. This ride included the officials of the Department of Transportation, and Walter Washington, the former Mayor of Washington, D.C. Most of my co-workers were about the same age and we found we had a lot in common. We enjoyed talking together, discussing our families and our similar interests. Again, I met and befriended some wonderful people (Carlyta Smith, Shirley Jones, Stephanie (Stevie) Watermier, Joan Bauerlein, and Delores Lynch) whose friendships have lasted over the years. I spent the last fourteen years of my public service career in several positions within the Department of Justice (DOJ), Office of Justice Programs (OJP). My service began in the Personnel Office, followed by the Office of Operations Support and lastly to the Equal Employment Opportunity Staff, Office for Civil Rights.

In 1984, under the direction of the OJP's first Assistant Attorney General, Lois Haight Herrington, I was selected to fill the position of EEO Specialist. Lois was a woman who was admired and respected by most employees for her management style and the special way she made everyone feel that their contribution to the mission of the agency was an important one. I admired her for her professionalism, love of family and the kindness she displayed with her employees. To this day, I treasure the Bible she gave me because it is the Bible that she used during her swearing-in ceremony as Assistant Attorney General. She said to me, "This Bible is special and I want you to have it because you are special to me." The Bible is autographed by her friend, former President Ronald Reagan. During Lois' tenure as Assistant Attorney General, she started the agency's first Bible study, of which I was a part. Our weekly meetings were held in her Conference Room and the attendees were a mix of the work force. The Bible study was conducted by Reverend Neal Avent, an agency employee. I learned much and met so many people working with Lois. I recall many days sitting at my desk when Lois would walk rapidly out of her office, stop in front of me and say, "I'd like you to go with me to a reception on Capitol Hill this evening." Other times she would say, "I need you to help me make plans for a reception in my conference room this evening." One thing I learned how to do was to be spontaneous. I never knew what my day would be like, working for Lois, but I knew it would always be interesting. In 1984, Lois invited me, along with some other agency employees, to attend a Rose Garden White House ceremony to witness the Victims of Crime Bill being signed into law.

Richard Abel (Rick) served as the Deputy Assistant Attorney General for OJP. After Lois left OJP, Rick became the Acting Assistant Attorney General. On December 3, 1986, Rick appointed me to the position of Equal Employment Opportunity Officer with full responsibility for managing the agency's EEO/Affirmative Employment Program. The EEO community within the Department of Justice worked as a team. Later, Kathleen Kennedy Townsend, currently Maryland's Lieutenant Governor, became the Deputy Assistant Attorney General. I had the pleasure of working with her on many agency projects. She was extremely supportive of equal employment opportunity within the agency and also supportive of me. This position enriched my life by allowing me to meet and work with such people as Janice Nance, Lois Salcedo, Rosa Washington, William (Bill) Adams, Sheila Monroe and others, too many to mention by name.

Working for the Department of Justice was both challenging and rewarding. However, there were many ironies working in the Equal Employment Opportunity Program. It did not take me long to realize that I was in a position that could easily cause me a lot of mental anguish and emotional stress. I found myself questioning the fairness of many decisions made by the Office of Personnel, even a decision effecting a promotion for me.

Prior to my appointment as the EEO Officer, the position was classified at the GS 14 grade level. When a request for my promotion was submitted to the Office of Personnel, it was denied even though the Position Description clearly stated additional duties had been added. The

Office of Personnel, through a Classification Desk Audit, denied my request stating the position fell a few points short of warranting the GS-14 grade level. I challenged their findings, but was unsuccessful in my efforts. Consequently, I never received the GS-14, and believe it was unfair.

Working with many of the summer interns from Howard University and other institutions of higher learning was rewarding. Angela LaCroix, then a student at the University of Maryland, was my first intern. She and I worked well together, until she graduated and moved on to a permanent job. Another highlight of my job as the EEO Officer, was to work with organizations, such as the National Organization of Black Law Enforcement Executives (NOBLE), National Association of Blacks in Criminal Justice (NABJC), National Council of LARAZA, League of Latin American Citizens (LULUC), National Association for Equal Opportunity in Higher Education (NAFEO) and others. I met an esteemed co-worker, Mercedes Maynor Faulcon, Assistant United States Attorney, from Nashville, Tennessee, during the National Association for the Advancement of Colored People (NAACP) Conference in Nashville, Tennessee. We have maintained a mutual friendship since our meeting.

In addition to the EEO Program responsibilities, I was assigned the task of establishing an educational outreach program with a local school. Directly under Attorney General Dick Thornburg and his Special Assistant, William (Bill) Lucas, through the Department's Legal Advocates in Education Program, I developed and implemented a Department of Justice, Office of Justice Programs' agency/school partnership with Orr Elementary School. The principal was Lawrence Boone and the Assistant Principal was Kia Garnett. I arranged for Orr students to participate in the agency's annual Black History Month celebrations where the students displayed their talents through songs and recitals. Teacher extraordinary, JoAnn Colbert, worked closely with me to plan and implement the programs. I enjoyed working with many other dedicated teachers and the fine students at Orr Elementary.

My journey through the federal government, especially the Department of Justice, was both challenging and rewarding. I enjoyed fourteen wonderful years. I did the best I could with the help of the Equal Employment Opportunity Staff, Justice Management Division and other components of the Department. Some key people included; Ted McBurrows, EEO Director for the DOJ, a soft-spoken gentleman for whom I have tremendous admiration and respect, Richard Tapscott, who duplicated Ted's supportive attitude, Violet Cromartie, Margaret Harding, Bureau of Prisons, Yvonne Makell, EEO Officer, United States Attorneys' Office, Barbara Lewis and Jim Getz, Drug Enforcement Assistant Administration, and Inez Alfonzo Lasso. I am thankful for my public service career and grateful for the interesting people who enriched my life on this part of my journey.

U.S. Department of Justice

Office of the Assistant Attorney General   *Washington, D.C. 20531*

Dear Barbara,

Thank you for all your help last Wednesday. You really contributed to a very successful and happy day for me personally. I'm so pleased to have you for a co-worker and friend.

Sincerely

Lois H. Herrington

4-013904U094024 04/04/85 ICS WA08186   WHSB
00177 MLTN VA 04/04/85

MS. BARBARA WOOD
OFFICE OF EQUAL EMPLOYMENT
OPPORTUNITY
633 INDIANA AVENUE, NW
WASHINGTON, DC 20531

ON BEHALF OF PRESIDENT REAGAN I WISH TO EXTEND TO YOU
AN INVITATION TO ATTEND A CEREMONY COMMEMORATING
VICTIMS OF CRIME WEEK ON FRIDAY, APRIL 19, AT 1:00 P.M.
IN THE ROSE GARDEN.

PLEASE RESPOND TO (202)456-2259 AND PROVIDE YOUR
SOCIAL SECURITY NUMBER AND DATE OF BIRTH IF YOU PLAN TO
ATTEND. ENTRANCE WILL BE AT THE VISITOR'S GATE ON EAST
EXECUTIVE AVENUE BEGINNING AT 12:30 P.M. YOU WILL BE
REQUIRED TO SHOW IDENTIFICATION AT THE GATE.

      ALFRED H. KINGON
      CABINET SECRETARY

23:12 EST

MGMCOMP

Motherland Experience

On September 29, 1993, I was blessed to be a part of a ten-day pilgrimage to West Africa, led by my pastor, Reverend Jonathan L. Weaver of Greater Mt. Nebo African Methodist Episcopal Church, Upper Marlboro, Maryland. At the beginning of the trip Pastor Weaver offered a prayer for a blessed trip, and a blessed and awesome one it was. Our tour group included Pastor Weaver and his mother Helen Weaver, Vertice Revels, Harvey Shelton, Maggie and Marvin Holmes, Ivory and Debra Foreman, Erin Plummer, my firstborn son, Claven Jr. and myself. I never dreamed, growing up in Bon Air, Virginia, that my journey through life would include a trip to the continent of Africa.

We departed John F. Kennedy International Airport on September 29th and arrived in Dakar, Senegal on Thursday, October 1st. The approximately seven-hour flight on Air Afrique, with its all black crew, was wonderful because everyone was extremely warm and courteous. The airplane was crowded and packed with people, luggage and packages, but it didn't matter because I was so happy to have this opportunity.

When I arrived in Senegal, I felt like I was at home. This trip cleared up a lot of misconceptions I had about Africa. A young Senegalese brother named Pape Alioune Gueye met our group. He was an experienced tour guide assistant. We also met some other friendly African brothers. Pape quickly became our friend, taking care of our needs, especially

89

translating betwewen French and English, and serving as our tour guide for our entire stay in the Motherland. Everyone was very impressed with Pape. He was a tall, slender, dark and very intelligent young man, well versed on most issues in the United States. Pape introduced us to his friend, Mamadou and other brothers, who owned their own tailoring business in Senegal. To my pleasure, I brought back many specially designed clothes by Mamadou. He designed outfits for many other members of our group as well. I admired his high level of professionalism, along with the friendly demeanor he and the other African people displayed in service to us.

We stayed at the Teranga Hotel in Dakar, the capital of Senegal. The hotel amenities were clean, but very basic. I believe the hotel had only about 20 double rooms total. There was a swimming pool and a small, but clean restaurant. I enjoyed meeting my Senegalese brothers and sisters at the Market Place in Senegal on our tour stops. We seemed to bond instantly with the people of Africa. On a city tour of Dakar, we saw the White House (Presidential Palace), a museum and Independence Square. To my surprise, I saw a street named in honor of Dr. Martin Luther King, Jr. Our tour included travel along Martin Luther King (MLK) Boulevard, the longest boulevard (three miles) and a trip to the University of Dakar.

After a day and a half in Senegal, our group departed from Dakar, making our way to the charming city of Banjul, The Gambia. This trip was a six-hour ride on a minibus traveling over mostly bumpy dirt roads. After the bus ride, we boarded a Barra Ferry for another half-hour ride over the Gambia River to Banjul. Just like the Senegalese, the Gambians were friendly and relaxed people. The Gambians' language is English, so we were able to communicate very well. In The Gambia, our accommodations were at the Atlantic Hotel, which was clean and comfortable, but also small. I enjoyed conversations with the native Gambians, experiencing evenings of traditional African entertainment and daily sunning and resting at poolside. We were invited by a friend of Pastor Weaver, Reverend Cole Njie, to a worship service at Wesley Methodist Church. Our pastor participated in the service by delivering greetings on behalf of Greater Mt. Nebo. After the service, our entire group was invited to dinner in the home of Reverend Cole Njie. She, her husband, and their four children welcomed us into their home with warm African hospitality. The plentiful dinner was a typical African meal of fish, millet, potato salad, rice, chicken, desserts and bissop (fruit drink). To have dinner in the home of the Njie family was very special, and our visit was made even more noteworthy when the four children sang songs of praise for us. The children of The Gambia were eager to receive the pencils, books, and pens we provided to them. These children, more than any of the others I had met, had a strong thirst for knowledge.

Our tour included a visit to the popular tapestry factory in Thies, where we saw firsthand the production of tapestry. En route to Thies, we visited the famous Rose Lake (Pink Lake) noted for its opaque pink mineral water. Many African people were seen doing their daily job of gathering salt from the lake to sell. It was interesting and heart-warming to see the many businesses and various occupations of brothers and sisters on the other side of the Atlantic Ocean. Woodcarving is a very popular occupation. Our tour included a visit to the famous Tie Dye Factory in Banjul, where we saw African people making dye and coloring fabrics. We were able to purchase the completed colorful fabrics. We also visited a Sand Painting Factory, where we saw lovely creative sand paintings done before our eyes. We purchased many of the paintings. I was highly impressed by the work of the people.

In addition to these interesting places, we visited a village called Juffure, off of the North bank of the Gambia River. I'd read about the village as written by the famous African American writer, Alex Haley, who traced his family ancestry back to the village of Juffure. In the mid 70's when I read Alex Haley's book, *Roots*, discussing the life and times of his enslaved ancestors, especially Kunta Kinte, I never thought I would one day walk in the village.

The most painful, yet informative and interesting part of the tour was the visit to Goree Island and the Historical Museum. Goree is known as the island of slavery and was originally used to sell African people to the Western World. Chief Curator, Joseph Ndiaye, informed us that millions of African men, women and children had been imprisoned at Goree. The African people were then transported across the Atlantic Ocean on ships to new lands. Once on new land they began new lives as slaves. The Goree experience started in the mid-15th century and continued for more than 300 years. Most of us were moved to tears as we heard the terrible stories of how African people were held for months in small concrete cells awaiting the voyage. There is a doorway at Goree called, "The Door of No Return." It is significant because as the African people made their final passage into slavery they walked through this small door, down a wooden plank and onto waiting ships, knowing they would never return to their homeland. African people who had once been kings and queens, were castrated and made into less than human beings. During this tour I felt the presence of my ancestors at Goree and it was an extremely emotional experience to hear how inhumanely they were treated.

Lastly, just before we departed the Motherland, teachers and others from the Society of History and Geography hosted a lovely farewell reception for us. The pilgrimage to West Africa was truly a blessing for me, and I realized that my African brothers and sisters are an extension of my family.

Retirement

It has been recorded in the Holy Bible: Romans 8:28,"... all things work together for the good of them that love God." All things did indeed work together for me to have reached this phase in my life.

In 1994 several federal government agencies offered employees with 50 years of age and twenty-five years of service, the opportunity to retire. I met both of the requirements and made the daring decision to retire. I shared my decision with my husband who was supportive. This decision brought closure to one area of my life and marked the beginning of another. I thought of the friends and close associates I had met and all that they meant to me. At the same time I was reflecting back I was looking ahead to plan other things for my life. It was a strange feeling to sign the retirement papers and end my progressive federal government career. I thought about the beginning of my career, as a GS-02 clerk and my progression to a GS-13 Program Manager and I realized that I hadn't made this journey through the government all by myself. It was with God's grace and mercy and the assistance from the many people who helped me along the way. On May 24, 1994, I found myself in the Great Hall of the Main Justice Building, at my retirement celebration, being honored by Attorney General Janet Reno, the first female to hold such rank, and other agency officials. The event was a beautiful testimony to my career as a public servant. This joyful celebration included family, friends and co-workers from throughout many federal agencies. What a great blessing!

On June 25, 1994, my retirement celebration culminated with a grand party at the Prince George's Ballroom in Landover, Maryland. The planning committee for my celebration included my younger sister, Gloria Quarles, close friend Deborah Smith, cousins, Wynee' Mitchell and Bobara Liles, and it was coordinated by my cousin, Anita Goode. The hostesses were family and friends: JoVonda Goode, Kirsten Reid, Patriece Nelson, Kim Johnson, Kima Watts, Phillicia Nelson, Jossolyn Edwards and Joy Quarles. Antonio Savage provided the music. Ronald Baker, Solid Image Photography, Upper Marlboro, Maryland, provided the videotaping. The Printing Clinic of Washington, D.C. prepared the program booklets. The tasty food was prepared and served in first-class style by Delbert Cross, owner of Adelis Catering, Washington, D.C, and his staff. Remarks were made by many of my friends and co-workers. Reverend Delores Lynch, Associate Minister, Covenant Baptist Church, Washington, D.C. and former federal government employee, talked about our work and business travels together. Constance Lykes, Confidential Assistant to the Under Secretary, Smithsonian Institution, shared the experience of how we met and our work experiences with Colonel Grimsley. During her remarks, she showed a gift that I had given her daughter over twenty five years ago - a little red velvet dress. The twenty five years represented the period of our friendship. The audience was stunned. Dr. Lorna Polk, Department of Education, White House Initiative on Historically Black Colleges and Universities, shared our experiences working together with the historically black colleges. Both Ted McBurrows, Director, Department of Justice, Equal Employment Opportunity Staff and Jeffery Hall, Equal Employment Opportunity Specialist, representing Inez Alfonzo Lasso, Director, of the Office for Civil Rights, Office of Justice Programs, gave remarks acclaiming my contribution to the agency's program. Also, remarks were made by Mrs. Mitchell, Orr Elementary School teacher, on behalf of the school's principal, Lawrence Boone applauding my dedication to the students. Bishop Clarence Groover, Pastor, Fisherman of Men Church, Washington, D.C., and his wife, Nettie, were also in attendance. Bishop Groover provided congratulatory remarks and talked about his long time friendship with my family. Also, Carolyn Williams, a DOJ co-worker and friend, along with her husband, Allen, made a special effort to share the time with me. Friends, Theresa Cone and Robin "Sugar" Williams, provided musical selections. Goddaughter, Tammi Palmer, served as the mistress of ceremonies.

A special warmth and genuine love permeated the festive evening. Approximately 200 family members, friends, neighbors and colleagues attended the elegant party. Family traveled from near and far to celebrate with me. My niece, Sandra Smith, her son Andre and my father-in-law, William Wood, Sr. traveled from Colonial Heights, Virginia; cousins, Sallie and Kima Watts, traveled from Petersburg, Virginia; Plum, his wife, Eva Sharpe and other family members traveled from Chester, Va; and Joyce Yelder traveled from Philadelphia, Pennsylvania to share the evening with me. With joy in my heart, I thanked everyone who contributed to this unforgettable event.

Immediately after retirement, I enrolled in Sojourner Douglass College (named in honor of two great leaders: Frederick Douglass and Sojourner Truth), Baltimore, Maryland, and graduated in 1996, Summa Cum Laude with a Bachelor of Arts Degree in Human and Social Resources. While attending college, I served as a member of the inaugural class of President William (Bill) Clinton's National Service Program, AmeriCorps;

whose members serve the community through a large network of programs in the areas of education, public safety, human needs and the environment. My service was in the area of education. AmeriCorps provided me the opportunity to serve others, earn a college stipend, and afforded me the pleasure of attending White House ceremonies with President Clinton.

Presently, I am cherishing the memories and taking pleasure in every facet of life.

This certificate is
presented to

Barbara B. Wood

upon your retirement from the
Government of the
United States of America
following _____ Thirty _____ Years
of loyal service

May 27 1994

_____

Janet Reno
Attorney General

ORR ELEMENTARY SCHOOL
WASHINGTON, D.C.
JUNE 25, 1994

OFFICE OF THE PRINCIPAL

TO BARBARA WOOD

ON THE OCCASION OF YOUR RETIREMENT CELEBRATION, I, AS PRINCIPAL
OF THE ORR ELEMENTARY SCHOOL IN WASHINGTON, D.C., SINCERELY WISH
YOU THE VERY BEST IN YOUR RETIREMENT. IT IS ALWAYS DIFFICULT TO
PART WITH THOSE WHO HAVE ENTHUSIASTICALLY DEDICATED THEIR LIVES
TO THE SERVICE OF OTHERS. AS YOU RETIRE FROM THE DEPARTMENT OF
JUSTICE, THE STAFF, PARENTS AND STUDENTS OF THE ORR ELEMENTARY
SCHOOL TAKE THIS OPPORTUNITY TO THANK YOU FOR HELPING US TO
NURTURE THE YOUNG MINDS AND ENCOURAGING THE DREAMS OF OUR
STUDENTS.

BARBARA, YOU ARE SPECIAL. YOUR GLOWING PERSONALITY AND RADIANT
SMILE WILL ALWAYS BE REMEMBERED BY THE ORR SCHOOL COMMUNITY.
YOUR DEDICATION TO PROVIDING THE SERVICES OF YOUR STAFF TO THE
CHILDREN OF ORR WILL ALWAYS BE REMEMBERED AND APPRECIATED.
SPECIAL PEOPLE LIKE YOU ARE SORELY NEEDED BY OUR YOUNG PEOPLE.
IT IS THROUGH THEIR VISION AND BELIEF IN CHILDREN THAT GOALS ARE
ACCOMPLISHED, CHARACTER IS DEVELOPED, AND LEADERS ARE MADE. YOU
HAVE BEEN FORTUNATE BECAUSE YOU HAVE TOUCHED THE LIVES OF SO MANY
CHILDREN.

AS YOU LEAVE THE DEPARTMENT OF JUSTICE, WE APPLAUD YOUR DEVOTION
TO PUBLIC SERVICE AND HOPE THAT YOUR RETIREMENT IS ENRICHED BY
FOND MEMORIES OF THE ORR SCHOOL COMMUNITY.

YOURS TRULY,

LAWRENCE E. BOONE
PRINCIPAL

THE WHITE HOUSE

WASHINGTON

September 9, 1996

Ms. Barbara Wood
10801 Sugar Maple Terrace
Upper Marlboro, Maryland   20772

Dear Barbara:

Thank you very much for participating in the "At the Table" discussion and for the feedback you provided. These round-tables are an extremely important part of our efforts to ensure that women's voices are heard on issues that affect their health, safety, and livelihood.

Your involvement is valuable to me and to my staff, and we will certainly keep the ideas you presented in mind in the months ahead. With your support, my Administration can continue our strong commitment to promoting the well-being of women across our country.

Sincerely,

THE WHITE HOUSE

WASHINGTON

March 27, 1995

Barbara Wood
10801 Sugar Maple Terrace
Upper Marlboro, Maryland 20772

Dear Barbara:

It is an honor to welcome you as a Member of the inaugural class of AmeriCorps. AmeriCorps is built on the tradition of national service established by programs such as the Peace Corps and the Civilian Conservation Corps. Like these programs, AmeriCorps provides opportunity while demanding responsibility and a commitment to confront and solve our nation's most pressing problems. I commend you for responding to this bold challenge.

You and more than 20,000 other AmeriCorps Members are making a difference by bringing emergency care to areas that have suffered from natural disaster, revitalizing inner-city neighborhoods, walking the beat with police, teaching in crowded classrooms, building homes for working families, and restoring our country's natural resources. You have accepted the responsibility to get things done on a local level and to learn from people of all different backgrounds. And you are creating common ground that all of us — as a nation — can build upon.

I am committed to making AmeriCorps a long-term success, and your input will help to achieve this goal. I want to know about the challenges you are facing and how you are meeting them; about how you are affecting the people and the communities you serve; and about how your work with AmeriCorps has changed you as an individual and as a citizen. Please take a moment to write to me at The White House, The AmeriCorps Program, 1600 Pennsylvania Avenue, Washington, D.C. 20502.

When we launched AmeriCorps in September, I asked three basic questions: What is right? What is wrong? And what are we going to do about it? As an AmeriCorps Member, you are doing what is right. You have shouldered enormous responsibility for yourself, for your neighbors, and for our nation. You represent what is best about America, and I look forward to hearing from you.

Sincerely,

Bill Clinton

EPILOGUE

I've written this book to share my life as openly as possible, staying focused on the things that were most important in shaping my character and my life's direction. I am sure there are some things that I have overlooked in spite of the many interviews with family and friends. Some things about my life will remain forever gone. With God's help , I have written this book, with honesty and love for all.

My life has been tremendously blessed through the highs and the lows. As the middle child, growing up feeling overlooked by my parents, and often left out of play by my siblings, I quickly found fulfillment by doing things to make myself happy. From these childhood experiences, I learned how to take charge of my life.

I believe most parents unintentionally treat their children differently by order of their birth and this treatment plays an important role in shaping the child's personality.

As an adult, my middle child position is the same, but instead of being overlooked, I am now looked upon as the centering guide in most family matters (symbolic of the middle child position). I'm usually the family member who is called upon for advice, planning and assistance. I deeply love my family and feel a closeness to them that deepens with time. It's not what I have done or where I've been, but it's who I am, the middle child.

Part Four

The Story in Pictures

Maternal grandfather, Cannon Hayes, standing in his yard in Amelia County, Virginia. Photo probably taken during the 1930s.

Parents, Roger Lee and Beulah Hayes Booker. Photo taken in mid 1970s.

Top: Mount Nebo Baptist Church Sunday School Class-1952.
Barbara, far right on the front row. Lower photo: Mt. Nebo
Baptist Church, photo taken in 1997.

NEW HOMEMAKERS OF AMERICA

Top photo: Barbara seated as secretary with the New Homemakers of America Club, Carver High School (1959 Yearbook photo). Lower left: Barbara, age 15. Lower right: Barbara and friend John Hardy Jr., photo taken in 1958.

Top photo: Carol's wedding (oldest sister), in 1958; Barbara, far left, and high school classmates, Phoebe and Shirley, as brides-maid. Lower left: Barbara and Claven's first photo together, in 1960 at G. C. Murphy, Richmond, Va.
Lower right: Barbara next to her first car, a 1963 Ford Falcon.

Top photo: Our first family photo taken in 1965 in our home. Lower left: Husband and sons, Claven, Claven Jr. and Calvin in Atlantic City, photo taken in 1969. Lower right: Goddaughter Tammi, her mother Jeanette and sister La Tanya, photo taken in 1977.

Top photo: Claven Jr.'s graduation from
Prince George's Community College;
parents Barbara and Claven Sr.

Center right: Tammi at her graduation
from Alabama StateUniversity, with
Barbara and granddaughter Carmela.

Lower left: Calvin's graduation from
Bladensburg High School (left to right)
Claven Jr., Calvin, Christine, Barbara,
and Claven Sr.

Top left: Claven Jr.'s graduation photo, Bladensburg High
School, 1979. Top right: Calvin's graduation photo, Bladensburg
High School, 1981. Lower left: Tammi as Miss ASU, photo
taken in 1991. Lower right: Tammi and Dr. Leon Howard,
President Alabama State University, at her graduation in 1991.

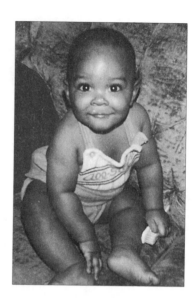
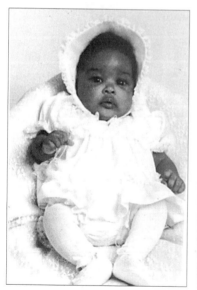
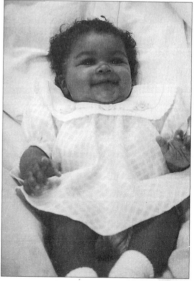

Top left: Claven and his family in 1990, wife Christine, Lil Calvin and Carmela. Top right: Lil Calvin; Lower left: Carmela; Lower right: Catarina. (Barbara's grandchildren at four months old).

Top center: Lil Claven, age fourteen. Lower left: Carmela, age ten.
Lower right: Catarina, age two.

Top photo: Barbara and Claven, photo taken in 1980 on a cruise to Bermuda celebrating twenty years of marriage. Lower photo: Barbara and Claven, photo taken at the 30th Reunion of Carver High School Class of 1960 in Richmond, Va.

Top photo: National Institutes of Health typing pool, Barbara's first place of employment in the federal government, photo taken in 1962. Lower left: Barbara and Attorney General Lois Haight Herrington in 1986. Lower right: Barbara, Deputy Assistant Attorney General Richard (Rick) Abell and Director, Bureau of Justice Statistics, Steven Schlussinger. Photos taken at the U.S. Department of Justice.

Top photo: Barbara in her official capacity at the U.S. Department of Justice, photo taken at a Special Emphasis Program in 1992. Lower left: Barbara and Attorney General Janet Reno at the Department of Justice in 1993. Lower right: Deputy Assistant Attorney General Kathleen Kennedy Townsend, District Attorney Eric Holder, and Orr Elementary School students at a Black History Month Celebration, U.S. Department of Justice.

Top photo: Greater Mt. Nebo A.M.E. Church tour group, and sisters and brothers in West Africa during our 1993 visit. Barbara, 3rd from the right on the back row. Lower photo: Barbara and siblings: Carol and James in front front, Barbara, in the middle, Floyd and Gloria in back. Photo taken in 1995 courtesy of cousin, Arnita Goode.